Discovering Pathways To Prayer

Msgr. David E. Rosage

LIVING FLAME PRESS
BOX 74 LOCUST VALLEY, N.Y. 11560

All scripture quotations are from the *New American Bible*.

Nihil Obstat: Rev. Peter Chirico, SS. S.T.D., *Censor Librorum*

Imprimatur: Rev. Bernard J. Topel, D.D., Ph.D., Bishop of Spokane

Cover: Robert Manning

Published by: Living Flame Press / Locust Valley / New York 11560

Copyright 1975: David E. Rosage

ISBN: 0-914544-08-x

Printed in the United States of America.

Introduction

I owe much to Monsignor Rosage's spiritual insights and guidance. This gem of a book is for God's "little" people who know their need of God, who hunger for Him and place their trust in Him.

It is so obvious that God is calling people to deepen their union with Him in prayer. There is a growing hunger for prayer in our times. Msgr. Rosage's *Discovering Pathways to Prayer* is the fruit of his own personal communion with the Lord and of God teaching him through the thousands of people he has guided in retreats and on-going spiritual direction.

May it reach millions and keep them open to the Lord who loves them, wants to communicate Himself to them and deepen His life and joy in them.

Armand M. Nigro, S.J.

Assoc. Prof. of Theology & Philosophy
Gonzaga University, Spokane, Washington

Preface

In these exciting days of renewal God is calling us into the desert that He may speak to our hearts. He is inviting us through prayer into a more intimate and personal relationship with Him. The time spent alone with God in prayer brings us to a richer and fuller awareness of His abiding presence with us and within us.

Prayer is a gift. Our reaction to a gift must be twofold: we must willingly and humbly accept the gift, and secondly, we must graciously show our appreciation by using the gift for the purpose for which it was intended. As we humbly accept His gift, we are able to enter into a deeper prayer experience with God, our Father. This experience of His love is most rewarding.

Our atmosphere is charged with radio and television signals. These are beyond the range of our normal hearing and vision. To enjoy these signals we must have the proper antennae. Likewise, God is present with us always and everywhere. In order to focus on His loving presence we need the antennae of a quiet, listening prayer posture. This posture is already prayer.

Discovering Pathways to Prayer is an attempt to point out some of the ways leading into a prayerful and personal union with God, our Father. This book is not intended to be a learned treatise or a theological presentation on prayer. It is rather a gleaning of some thoughts that I have been privileged to share with others in retreats, prayer workshops, spiritual direction and other priestly ministry. Many of these people have enriched my life with the thoughts on prayer they have so graciously shared with me.

This book is only an outline of some pathways leading into prayer. It is intended for those of us who are still struggling to find the pathways, rather than for those whom God has so blessed and gifted that they have already made progress on these pathways.

I am deeply grateful to all those magnanimous people whom God has sent into my life and who have so enriched it as they taught me much about prayer. My saintly parents, my teachers, my brothers in the priesthood, are in the vanguard of the vast army of persons who have helped me with my prayer.

If this book, through the power of the Holy Spirit, draws one person into the desert of a prayer posture so that God may speak to his heart, then may God be praised.

David E. Rosage

Contents

Chapter One

Prayer Is Gift

"Lord, teach us to pray" (Luke 11:1).

Some years ago the saintly Pope John asked the entire Christian world to pray that God would renew His signs and wonders in our times. God has heard our prayer and is granting our requests with a fabulous outpouring of His Holy Spirit. One of the ways in which God is renewing His signs and wonders in our day is by filling us with His Holy Spirit, Who creates in us the desire for prayer.

This hunger for prayer is really a longing for a more personal union with God. Many of us are searching for richer prayer experiences. We are seeking an experiential awareness of the presence of God in our lives. This desire is in itself a gift from God. St. Paul minces no words about this fact when he says, "It is God who, in his good will toward you, begets in you any measure of desire or achievement" *(Philippians 2:13).*

God is drawing us into a closer relationship. Because of this, we are no longer satisfied merely "to say prayers" but we are searching for a much broader dimension in our prayer life than mere recitation. This fact is attested to by the number of houses of prayer which are springing into existence. Special retreats, institutes and workshops on prayer are becoming popular. Courses in Sacred Scripture are emphasizing the Word of God as a key source of prayer. All this is the work of the Holy Spirit in our midst. Again it is the Holy Spirit who speaks to us through St. Paul, "It is not that we are entitled of ourselves to take credit for anything. Our sole credit is from God" *(II Corinthians 3:5)*. Prayer, too, is a gift from God. Only God can pray in us and teach us how to pray.

One day Jesus was deeply engrossed in prayer. His disciples were observing Him intently. As He was in communion with His Father, they must have noticed the peace, joy and the serenity which radiated from His face. They longed for that same experience. They turned to their Master and begged, "Lord, teach us to pray" *(Luke 11:1)*. In the wake of what God is trying to effect in us, we, too, must beg: "Lord, teach us to pray."

Jesus Prayed

Jesus taught us a great deal about prayer both by His Word and His example. On many occasions, throughout His public life, He retired to a lonely spot (an olive grove, a mountaintop, a desert place), to be alone with His Father in prayer. The Evangelists remind us that He frequently spent time in prayer prior to many of the important events of His life.

Before Jesus selected the twelve who were to be His apostles, He spent the whole night in prayer. "Then he went out to the mountain to pray, spending the whole night in communion with God" *(Luke 6:12ff)*. We can be certain that Jesus did not spend the night with His Father reviewing the list of potential candidates for this high office. Rather, we can be certain that much time was spent praising and thanking His Father for the glory of His kingdom which was being established in the world.

Likewise, Jesus felt the need of His Father's support before He began a new day. "Rising early the next morning, he went off to a lonely place in the desert; there he was absorbed in prayer" *(Mark 1:35)*. Jesus also wanted to thank His Father for the signs and wonders which had been performed the evening before when "they brought Him all who were ill and those possessed by demons" and He cured them all.

The prophet Isaiah assures us that God's ways are not our ways, nor His thoughts our thoughts. Jesus praised His Father for His unique way of doing things. Listen to His prayer: "Father, Lord of heaven and earth, to you I offer praise; for what you have hidden from the learned and the clever you have revealed to the merest children. Father, it is true. You have graciously willed it so" *(Matthew 11:25-26ff)*.

Jesus taught us, while praying in the garden at Gethsemane, the value of acceptance and conformity to the will of the Father. Jesus shuddered at the thought of His forthcoming rejection and cruel passion, yet He prayed with resignation, "My soul is troubled now, yet what should I say — Father, save me from this hour? But it was for this that I came to this hour. Father, glorify your name!" Then a voice came from the sky: "I have glorified it, and will glorify it again" *(John 12:27ff)*.

When His hour had come and the forces of darkness were moving relentlessly upon Him, Jesus prayed, "My Father, if it is possible let this cup pass me by. Still, let it be as you would have it, not as I" *(Matthew 26:39)*.

11

Jesus taught us a powerful prayer in preparation for the coming of His Kingdom, the Lord's Prayer, "Your Kingdom come, Your will be done" *(Matthew 6:10)*.

Jesus wanted the prayerful support of His friends when He faced the dreadful agony in the garden. His disappointment at their failure to respond in His hour of need is quite evident. "So you could not stay awake with me for even an hour?" *(Matthew 26:40)*. Do we hear that plea deep in our own hearts? "Could you not stay awake with me for even an hour?" Jesus really did teach us a lot about prayer.

Our Role

There are two important aspects to prayer. The first concerns what we must do to enter into a prayer experience. Our role in coming to prayer is called the ascetical approach. This is the first step in our preparation for prayer. There is very little we can do. We can bring ourselves before the Lord and strive to open ourselves completely to what He wants to accomplish in us. In other words, we must place ourselves in a position that allows God to pray in us. If we want to enjoy the warmth and the brightness of the sun, we must go out-of-doors and place ourselves into a position where we can enjoy the rays of the sun. Similarly, in prayer we bring ourselves before the Lord to permit Him to act in us.

Of ourselves we cannot pray. The great Apostle of the Gentiles makes this quite clear, when he explains the action of the Holy Spirit within us. "The Spirit, too, helps us in our weakness, for we do not know how to pray as we ought; but the Spirit himself makes intercession for us . . . for the Spirit intercedes for the saints as God himself

12

wills" *(Romans 8:26-27)*.

Once I observed a hawk being supported by an updraft of wind which blew against a canyon wall and then went straight up. The hawk had put itself into a position where it could take full advantage of the updraft and be held aloft without exercising any energy on its part. This observation suggested a potential prayer posture.

Sailing affords another good illustration of a prayer posture. We can prepare for sailing by unmooring the boat and setting the sails, but only God can provide the wind to make our day of sailing a thrilling delight. For, if there is not even a breath of wind, we will go nowhere.

Let us consider another example. One of the first requisites in learning to swim is to relax in the water. As we relax, we are amazed how buoyant the water is and how much it supports us. Similarly, relaxation is a prerequisite for prayer. Our hearts must be serene and tranquil in God's presence. We must permit His power and presence to take over. Prayer is turning our attention to God and disposing our souls for His action in us.

Our receptivity to God's work in us can be illustrated by observing a gentle rain falling on a newly plowed field. The looseness of the soil immediately absorbs the drops of rain as they nourish and enrich it. On the other hand, if that same gentle rain falls on a rock, it wets the rock but most of the rain bounces off. Our openness to God's action in us is the first requisite for prayer. God is so good. He even considers our attempt to be receptive as prayer.

God's Role

The second aspect of prayer is God's action in us, the mystical portion. This is a pure gift from

God. It does not depend on our efforts exclusively. We can prevent God's action in us, but we cannot induce it at will.

When we enjoy a sense of God's presence, when we are aware of His loving concern, this is God's action in us. Again this is gift. Jesus said clearly and emphatically, "Apart from me you can do nothing" *(John 15:5)*. Each day the truth of this axiom is impressed upon us. When we fail, we are reminded of these words of Jesus and we turn to Him to begin once again. The same is true of our prayer. When we try to pray and nothing seems to happen, we must remind ourselves that God will pray in us as He wills. God operates within us in prayer, provided we are open to His presence and power. When God brings us to an awareness of His presence, when we experience His loving concern and strive to respond to His indwelling, then we are praying.

Prayer is a gift because the very source of our prayer is Gift. The dynamic behind our prayer is the Holy Spirit. Without Him we cannot pray. Jesus promised us that He would not leave us orphans, but He would remain with us through the power of His Holy Spirit. Furthermore, He urged us to ask for the outpouring of the Holy Spirit. Here are His words, "So I say to you, 'Ask and you shall receive; seek and you shall find; knock and it shall be opened to you.' For whoever asks, receives; whoever seeks, finds; whoever knocks, is admitted. What father among you will give his son a snake if he asks for a fish, or hand him a scorpion if he asks for an egg? If you, with all your sins, know how to give your children good things, how much more will the heavenly Father give the Holy Spirit to those who ask him" *(Luke 11:9-13)*.

Not only did Jesus encourage us to ask the Father to fill us with His Spirit, but He also promised that He would personally pray with and for us. The evening before He died, Jesus and His Apostles were gathered in the Upper Room. He was saying His farewell to them by encouraging them and reassuring them that He was not going to leave them orphans, but would return to them through the power of His Holy Spirit. On this memorable evening, Jesus was not thinking about the hatred, envy and intrigue which were moving upon Him. He was thinking about us. He promised to send His Spirit to us.

"I will ask the Father and he will give you another Paraclete — to be with you always: the Spirit of truth whom the world cannot accept, since it neither sees him nor recognizes him; but you can recognize him because he remains with you and will be within you" *(John 14:16-17)*.

God is always faithful to His promises, and we know that He has given us His Spirit. Jesus said that His Spirit would be with us "always." He also said that the Spirit is "with" us and "within" us. That is why St. Paul could say to his Corinthian converts, "Are you not aware that you are the temple of God, and that the Spirit of God dwells in you?" *(I Corinthians 3:16)*. The Holy Spirit is dwelling "with" us and "within" us. This is a special Gift from the Father to His children.

Jesus promised us, furthermore, that " . . . the Paraclete, the Holy Spirit whom the Father will send in my name, will instruct you in everything, and remind you of all that I told you" *(John 14:26)*. This Holy Spirit will instruct and guide us in everything. It also means that the Holy Spirit will teach us how to pray.

Prayer is a gift and the very origin of our prayer is the Holy Spirit. St. Paul makes that unmistakably clear when he writes, "The Spirit too helps us in our weakness, for we do not know how to pray

15

as we ought; but the Spirit Himself makes **intercession** for us with groanings that cannot be expressed in speech. He who searches hearts knows what the Spirit means, for the Spirit intercedes for the saints as God himself wills" *(Romans 8:26-27).* The Holy Spirit prays in us and teaches us how to pray by creating in us the appropriate attitudes for prayer.

Abba Father

Before we can enter into real prayer we must have the correct concept of God. He is not a God who is far removed from us. Nor is He a God who created the universe and set everything in motion and then withdrew to let everything take care of itself. Someone has said: "If God seems far away, whom do you think moved?" God obviously did not.

God is our loving and kind Father who is concerned about us at every moment of the day. The Holy Spirit formulates within us the proper attitude toward God. Listen to Paul explaining this truth: "All who are led by the Spirit of God are sons of God. You did not receive a spirit of slavery leading you back into fear, but a spirit of adoption through which we cry out 'Abba!' (that is, Father). The Spirit himself gives witness with our spirit that we are children of God" *(Romans 8:14-16).*

The Holy Spirit teaches us that God is our Abba — our Daddy. If He is our Abba, then there is no place for fear in our hearts. We can approach Him as our loving Father. As children we can climb into His lap and let Him love and protect us. John says, "Love has no room for fear; rather, perfect love casts out all fear" *(I John 4:18).*

Secondly, if the Father really loves us, we can come to Him in perfect surrender. We can trust

16

Him. Nothing will upset us. Nothing can harm us because our loving Father is protecting us at every moment of the day. Jesus says, "Do not let your hearts be troubled. Have faith in God and faith in me" *(John 14:1)*.

Thirdly, the Spirit teaches us that our response to a loving Abba is to do whatever He asks of us. Jesus taught us how to do the will of His Father. Jesus loved His Father and because of this infinite love, He wanted only to do the Father's will. We prove our love for our Father by striving to discover and do His will. This creates an ideal attitude for prayer. Instead of coming to prayer to ask God our Father for what we want, we come to Him asking: "What is it you want of me?" This is real prayer.

Jesus the Way

The Holy Spirit teaches us how to pray by helping us to acquire the mind of Jesus. St. Paul tells us: "Your attitude must be that of Christ" *(Philippians 2:5)*. In his letter to the Ephesians Paul is quite imperative about this when he says, "Acquire a fresh, spiritual way of thinking. You must put on the new man created in God's image, whose justice and holiness are born of truth" *(Ephesians 4:23-24)*. And in another Epistle Paul does not mince words: "If anyone does not have the Spirit of Christ, he does not belong to Christ" *(Romans 8:9)*.

In order to pray well, we must have the mind of Jesus in us. We can acquire the mind of Jesus by spending time in prayer, especially the prayer of listening, where we listen with all our hearts to what Jesus is saying to us in His Word.

One aspect of the mind of Jesus which it is essential to have if we wish to pray, is an attitude of respect and love for every person. Jesus was able to reach out in love to everyone. He recognized in every person a child of His Father. Whether they were friends or enemies, Jesus respected and loved them.

In our lives there can be many impediments to prayer. Most of us have difficulty relating to other people, especially those with whom we have to deal on a daily basis. Resentments, anger, dislikes, envies, jealousies and a host of other attitudes are huge roadblocks to prayer. The Holy Spirit is convicting us of many of these barriers and is showing us that we cannot learn to pray until we try to remove these impediments.

The Spirit is enabling us to reach out in loving forgiveness to others. He is healing many of these interpersonal relationships so that He can form the mind of Jesus in us. The Spirit is helping us to accept, as Jesus did, everyone who crosses our path. This gives us a new freedom — a freedom which is the result of having the mind of Christ and a freedom which is necessary and basic to prayer.

Another area in which the Spirit is leading us to a correct attitude in prayer is in the realm of material attachments. Jesus was totally detached from the material things of this world. He enjoyed an interior freedom which gave Him the ability to use the goods of this world without becoming enslaved by them. Jesus was able to say of Himself, "The foxes have lairs, the birds in the sky have nests, but the Son of Man has nowhere to lay his head" *(Matthew 8:20)*. This freedom is a posture which is fundamental to a real life of prayer.

As a true follower of Jesus, St. Francis of Assisi enjoyed the material things of this world because he was completely detached from them. He was totally free. When we are unduly attached, we have many concerns and worries. When we do not cling to anything, we have a freedom which is the threshold to a deeper union with God in prayer.

Jesus encouraged us in the pursuit of this freedom when He advised us, "Your heavenly Father knows all that you need. Seek first his kingship over you, his way of holiness, and all these things will be given you besides" *(Matthew 6:32-33)*. This total dependence upon God is another prerequisite to authentic prayer.

The Holy Spirit is teaching us another all-important truth about Jesus. He is teaching us that Jesus is Lord. This brief formula was the first profession of faith among the early Christians. It is probably the most difficult prayer in all the world.

To pray "Jesus is Lord" means an unconditional and unreserved giving of ourselves to Jesus. He must be Lord of our thoughts, Lord of our words, Lord of our activities. There can be no area of our life which does not belong to Jesus the Lord. No decision is made without consulting Him; no task undertaken without asking His help and guidance. The words "Jesus is Lord" may come glibly from our lips, but to live out this confession in everything we do is far more difficult. A friend once said, "It is easy to talk your talk, but it is much harder to walk your talk." Here again the Holy Spirit comes to our rescue for, " . . . no one can say: 'Jesus is Lord,' except in the Holy Spirit" *(I Corinthians 12:3)*. Only through the power of the Holy Spirit can we pray this prayer, "Jesus is Lord." And only through His power can we live this profession of faith. This, too, is a gift.

The Spirit Prays

The Holy Spirit teaches us how to pray by praying within us. He Himself prays in us and through us to the Father. The Spirit, dwelling within us, unites our spirit to His Spirit and thus prays in us and through us to the Father. This makes our prayer less active, because we learn to listen more and more to the Spirit praying in us.

The Desert Fathers described Christian prayer as listening more deeply within ourselves to the prayer Jesus utters through His Spirit to the Father. In this sense our prayer becomes more passive. We are content simply to rest in His presence. Gradually, we begin to realize that we are not doing the praying, but the Spirit Himself is praying in us.

Prayer is our relationship to God. If we are striving to live, move and act with an awareness of God's abiding presence at all times, we are praying. When we are convinced that every heartbeat is a gift from God, that every hair on our head is counted, we are praying. This awareness and conviction is prayer.

Since prayer is our relationship with God, we can understand Paul's injunction " . . . never cease praying" *(I Thessalonians 5:17)* and " . . . persevere in prayer" *(Romans 12:12)*. We cannot be constantly addressing our thoughts and words to God in prayer, but our attitudes and mentality can always be prayerfully God oriented.

Since prayer is a gift, it behooves us to be grateful for that gift, and that, too, is prayer.

Chapter Two

Prayer Is Listening

"Oh, that today you would hear his voice: Harden not your hearts . . . " (Psalm 95:7-8).

Prayer is our communication with God, but it is also God's communication with us. Communication is a two-way street. To enjoy good communication with another person we must speak, but above all, we must listen and "there's the rub." Listening is an art which is by no means easy. We hear a great deal but we listen very seldom.

To listen is much more difficult than to speak. When we speak we are the center of attention. We enjoy this. However, when we listen, the other person becomes the center of attention and that is much more demanding. To listen means that we place ourselves totally in the position of the other person. We must try to experience the feelings which he is experiencing. This requires great effort and renunciation on our part, especially if we listen for any great length of time. It means that we must empty ourselves in order to be filled with the other person.

Jesus is the Master-listener. He has no selfish

concerns. Jesus empties Himself so that He can give Himself completely to us. Since we are His primary concern, He is a listener par excellence.

In communications we are not always concerned with equal time. In order to have effective communications the person who has the message of greater import should be given more time. Now in prayer, it should be obvious Who has the more important message; hence our prayer time should be spent mostly in listening to God. One of the common errors in prayer is the assumption that we must do most of the talking. On the contrary, prayer is listening in the very depth of our being. It is listening but it is much more. It is listening not only with our ears but with our whole body: with our eyes, our touch, and especially with our heart. In its broader meaning, listening implies being open to what God wants to do in us and also being ready to respond to God.

It is exciting to discover how many times the word "listen" is used in Sacred Scripture. The word we find most frequently in the Bible is the name of God, under one or more of His many titles. Running a close second is the word "listen" or its synonyms: "hearken," "attend," "pay attention," "open your ears," "hear and heed" and a host of others. "Listen" is used so frequently that we can be sure that God is trying to tell us something. Yes, listening is vitally important in our prayer life.

Our understanding of God has an important effect on our listening. If God is a wholly transcendent Being Who spoke of old but is now silent, He becomes the Law-Giver, the Judge, the Ruler, the Omnipotent One and prayer becomes for us an empty formula, a duty to perform or a dry ritual. Fortunately God is not only a transcendent God; He is also an immanent God. He is continually manifesting Himself to us which is the basis of our personal relationship with Him. We know God only inasmuch as He wishes to reveal Himself to us, in a totally gratuitous manner and our ongoing dialogue with Him is true prayer. Jesus said, " . . . no one knows the Father but the Son — and anyone to whom the Son wishes to reveal him" *(Matthew 11:27)*.

Revelation is a living, continuous and ever present historical fact. God continues to reveal Himself unwaveringly, unhesitatingly, unreservedly and consistently throughout history and not only at one given moment of time. Revelation has not ended and indeed never will end as long as God continues to deal personally with us and manifest His presence in human history. What consolation and joy this brings into our life, knowing that God is ever present to us and will continue to make Himself known in our everyday situations.

God does even more. He does not give Himself to us simply to be known, but that we might possess Him in a special way. By communicating with us, God does not give us *information* about Himself, but gives us *Himself*. Revelation then, is the living Word that the living God is addressing to the living members of His Body. For this we are deeply grateful and we praise Him daily for His Word and we must respond to it.

The priest Eli advised the young man Samuel to listen if the Lord spoke to him. When God called Samuel, he immediately responded, "Speak, Lord, for your servant is listening" *(I Samuel 3:9-10)*. The psalmist, too, begs us, "Oh, that today you would hear his voice; harden not your hearts . . . " *(Psalm 95:7-8)*.

A passage from the Old Testament tells us much about how God speaks to us. In the Book of Kings, it is related that God wanted to speak to the prophet Elijah. The inspired author tells us, "A strong and heavy wind was rending the mountains and crushing rocks before the Lord — but the Lord was not in the wind. After the wind there was an earthquake — but the Lord was not in the earthquake. After the earthquake there was fire — but the Lord was not in the fire. After the fire there was a tiny whispering sound . . . " *(I Kings 19:11-12)*. In this "tiny whispering sound" Elijah experienced God speaking to him. This "tiny whispering sound" is an image, but it describes well how God speaks to us, or how we experience God's voice.

In our eagerness to enter quickly and deeply into prayer, we often plunge right in and begin to thank God for some favor, or appraise Him of some situation, or simply ask Him to come and help us do our thing. We feel that we cannot sit or kneel in prayer and do nothing. Just waiting and listening with our whole being seems so impractical. With our pragmatic mentality, patiently waiting on the Lord seems such a waste of time. Yet in order to pray well, we must be willing to "waste time." The psalmist, too, reminds us, "Be still before the Lord," and also, "wait in patience." In these moments of restlessness, our prayer must be "slow me down, Lord," or, "quiet me, Lord."

As long as our focus is on ourselves, we will have difficulties-a-plenty in prayer. Our focus must be on God. He wants to speak to us. He wants us to listen in the quiet of our whole being and, only after we have listened intently, respond in our hearts.

Mary, the Mother of Jesus, is a perfect exemplar of listening. She committed her whole life to God, hence she was always completely receptive to the Word of God. Like Mary, we want to let all of God's message through so that our lives, like hers, might be fully in accord with God's will or preference. In this prayer posture we will find genuine joy.

Modern psychology is teaching us much about the art of listening. Some psychologists maintain that more is transmitted to a person by the pauses in our conversation than by our words. These pauses give the message a chance to penetrate the fiber of our being. If this is true, this tells us much about the importance of the listening-pauses in our prayer.

In the pastoral parable about the sower and the seed, Jesus teaches us the necessity of listening. "Let everyone who has ears attend to what he has heard" *(Luke 8:4-15)*. The Father, too, admonishes us to listen. When Jesus was transfigured on Mount Tabor before Peter, James and John, the Father spoke from the cloud and advised us, "This is my Son, my Chosen One. Listen to him" *(Luke 9:35)*.

It is not only startling, but even mysterious, when we consider that the transcendent God of heaven and earth wishes to communicate with us even though we are but tiny grains of sand in this immense universe. Incomprehensible as it may seem, it is true. God does want to communicate with us. He does not shout, nor does He force us to pause in our hurry-filled life, but He does invite us to "come by yourselves to an out-of-the-way place and rest a little" *(Mark 6:32)*. This "out-of-the-way place" may be the solitude of our own heart, our room, a mountaintop, a busy street. He assures us that He will speak to our heart as He reminds us through the prophet, "I will lead her into the desert and speak to her heart" *(Hosea 2:16)*.

It is not easy for us to comprehend the momentous truth that the transcendent God of heaven and earth, the Creator of the entire universe, wishes to communicate with us personally and individually. Yet it is true. God is a universal God, but He is also a personal God. He is concerned about every creature, but He is equally concerned about me as an individual. He is the transcendent God of heaven and earth, yet He makes Himself so immanent that He speaks to us through His "voiceless voice" within us.

Silence

Before we can really listen to God speaking to us, we must learn to be silent. Silence is not merely the abstention from verbal communication. There must also be the silence of the heart. God speaking to us through the psalmist invites us to "desist! and confess that I am God" *(Psalm 46:11)*.

Our subconscious mind is our memory computer. There, also, we house our habit-patterns. Each day our subconscious is bombarded with countless sensory images. This accentuates the importance of silence. Silence is making room for God in our lives. In silence God comes to us and clears away much of the debris blocking His way. God's presence is interiorized. We sit at His feet like Mary, listening, just listening. God then talks to us as to a friend. When we become silent, the Holy Spirit enters with His gift of wisdom for which we pray.

The prayer of listening can be compared to parking our car. It is not enough simply to drive our car into a parking space, we must also turn off the motor. Prayer is not merely pausing but also relaxing in silence in order to hear God speaking to our hearts.

God Speaks

In prayer our focus must be on God, not on ourselves. As we prayerfully listen to God, our heart is eager to respond. God uses many and various avenues to convey His message to us.

In the first place, God speaks to us through His Word as recorded in Sacred Scripture. We shall speak of this method of communication later.

God speaks to us through the liturgy. As we join our brothers and sisters in offering the Eucharistic Celebration, God sometimes brings us to a sense of solidarity. We may experience His Presence with us sacramentally especially during the precious moments of Holy Communion. Yes, God does communicate with us in the Holy Sacrifice of the Mass.

God spoke to me very powerfully while I was offering Mass on a special retreat for a group of handicapped people, some 40 of whom were in wheelchairs. It was a gorgeous day and Mass was planned for the outdoors under a canopy of oak trees. The altar was surrounded by a halo of wheelchairs. When I observed the joy on the faces of these handicapped people, I could almost feel the presence of God. Many of these people had not been to Mass for a long time. Some had not even been outside in the fresh air for many months. Their faces radiated the joy which filled their hearts as they shared in the Eucharistic Liturgy.

God spoke to me through those precious people. I realize that I have the privilege of offering Mass anytime I wish. I can offer it at any hour to suit my convenience. These people, who do not have that privilege, can participate in the Mass only rarely. This fact brought me to a realization of the unique privilege which was mine. God used this occasion to create in me a greater depth of gratitude. I have offered this august Sacrifice differently since that memorable day. I thank God for getting His message through to me.

Frequently God uses the events of our daily living to convey an important message to us. At the time of its occurrence an event may seem rather tragic. When we look back, after a certain period of time, we may discover that that specific event was a great blessing stemming from the providential concern of our loving Father. Other incidents in our life may serve as forceful reminders of God's paternal care for us, His children. If we pause to reflect for a moment, numerous events will come to mind which demonstrate God's love for us.

Many of us, I fear, departmentalize our lives. We work, we play, we pray. We so partition our lives that we are conscious of only one activity at a time. Prayer, on the contrary, should permeate our work and our play, just as play should be part and parcel of our work life and our prayer life. Unless God is part of my everyday activities, He is not part of my prayer life. Either He speaks to me at all times, or He doesn't speak to me at any time. We cannot control God's revelations. He reveals Himself to us *as* He pleases, *when* He pleases and in *the way* He pleases. Our job is to simply respond in love to all His manifestations.

God may reveal Himself in a strange, mystical way but this is not the usual method which He uses. God generally acts in our lives in a normal, delicate, almost imperceptible manner. He acts so gently, that unless we are attentive to His delicate ways, His presence can pass unnoticed and His inspiration unheard. We must empty ourselves of self in order to see God and to hear His Word. We will only hear Him in the peace and stillness of our innermost being.

If we have never experienced God's Self-revelation, or if we cannot hear God speaking plainly, it might be well to ask ourselves two questions.

First, are we sure that there is not something which He is plainly saying to us, and to which we are not giving ear? Are we prepared to hear whatever God may have to say to us, no matter what it may turn out to be? Can we honestly say that there is no voice now seeking to make itself heard, and to which we are not attending — perhaps even pretending to ourselves that we do not hear it? Is there within us a sense of dissatisfaction with our present way of living, or with some particular thing in our lives, or some interpersonal relationship about which we are bitter, and for one or another of these reasons are half suppressing God's communication? Perhaps we are stopping our ears because the task before us is distasteful, but God could be speaking to us about that very task at this very moment.

The second question which we should put to ourselves is this: if we have listened, have we obeyed? Scripture illustrates several instances where God's command to an individual or a group was not obeyed. God then discontinued His communication. Scripture warns us that we can receive no further revelation until we have not only listened attentively to His voice, but also acted upon the Word that we have already received.

God speaks to us through other people. He may use our spouse, our children, the person with whom we work, the neighbor next door or even a casual encounter with a stranger. God may send a person into our lives to support and encourage us at the very moment we need that encouragement. Another person may draw our attention to some fault or weakness. This, too, is God's way of bringing to our attention some areas where we need improvement.

While it is true that the experience of God communicating Himself is a very personal one, He also speaks to us through community. The vast majority of examples which Jesus gave about the nearness of God are concerned with the relationships between people. We live and work with the same people everyday. These day-after-day experiences with people may become rather routine and monotonous, yet if we are truly aware of God's movements, we shall be able to feel His touch or hear His inspiration during the mundane events of everyday living.

We may be able to experience God in a fleeting smile, or in a silent moment, or even working side by side with others. For a moment, at least, something is different because we have had an experience, or a glimpse, of the nearness of God. The result may be a strengthening of our faith, courage to continue our work, or the mere peace and joy of knowing that God is with us.

God also uses the mass media to communicate His message. A radio program may inspire us to thank God for our gift of hearing. A news item may remind us how badly our civil officials need our prayerful support. A television program may make us more aware of the suffering of our brothers and sisters halfway around the world. All these means are at God's disposal and He does employ them in trying to reach us.

How frequently, how forcefully and how eloquently God communicates Himself to us through visible creation. Viewing a celestial sunset, a teen-ager was heard to say: "Hurrah for God!" A tiny ant, a mighty tree, the smile of a child, a billowing cloud formation, an incomparable sunset and a snowcapped mountain all remind us of the creative goodness of God.

Yes, God does converse with us in many different ways but it is imperative that we listen. We are so apt to begin our prayer by addressing ourselves to God. We have so many things that we wish to talk over with Him. We need to inform Him of so many of our needs. Many of us often come to prayer in this way. Then as soon as we are finished, we leave our prayer time without giving God an opportunity to converse with us. We are so impatient that we do not want to waste time just sitting and waiting upon the Lord. We have become so work-oriented that we must be constantly productive. As long as our focus remains on ourselves we will have problems learning to pray.

In order to listen well, we must strip ourselves of all that is self. Our hopes and ambitions, our worries and anxieties must all be laid aside. The evil one will do his utmost to keep these before our minds. We can depend on that when we come to prayer.

Jesus said, "None of you can be my disciple if he does not renounce all his possessions" *(Luke 14:33)*. This is an excellent axiom for our prayer. We can be certain that Jesus was not speaking about material possessions only. Perhaps our most cherished possession is our own will, the program we have set up for ourselves that day, the goal we have set for ourselves. To pray well we must strip ourselves of all such "possessions."

In the Bible we find many examples of God stripping people of their "possessions" so that they will come to Him in a listening posture. When Moses led the Israelites out of Egypt into the desert, God wanted to impress upon them that He was their God and He wanted them to listen to Him. Accordingly He stripped them of everything — water, food, a fixed abode, comfortable security. They were not even permitted to make a covenant, for their own protection, with any other people.

Only after this "dispossession" were they able to listen to God.

We find a similar example in the life of St. Paul. On the road to Damascus God stripped Paul of everything. His Greek culture, his Jewish education, his Roman citizenship, all were of little value unless they were directed Godward. Before Saul would listen, however, God had to strip him of everything. He even permitted temporary blindness so that Saul could listen better. Once Saul began to listen, all these gifts were used for the greater glory of God.

At a workshop on prayer, a young man shared with us what God taught him about entering into prayer. He told us this story:

"When I was a small boy living on a farm, I wanted a twenty-two rifle and a bicycle. I prayed hard for both of these, but apparently God was not hearing my prayer for I didn't get either a rifle or a bicycle. I concluded that God was not answering my prayer because He could not hear me way up there in heaven.

"One day I got a great idea. It was bound to work. I loved to fly my kite down by the river which ran through our farm. There was nearly always a good wind down there, and my kite would soar up and up. My idea was to write a note and tie it on the tail of my kite, and then fly my kite as high as I could so that God could read my prayer.

"In my boyish excitement, I ran down to the river. I unfurled my kite to the breeze. The wind was perfect. It soared up and up and soon I was at the end of my string. The kite kept tugging on my hand like a fish on the end of a line. I looked up and, to my amazement, my kite wasn't nearly high enough. God still could not read my note. I began to cry. I loved my kite and I knew what I had to do, I cried and cried and then finally I let my kite go."

This is an ideal prayer posture. When we come before the Lord in prayer, we must come with open mind and heart and ask, "Lord, what do you want of me today?"

Speaking about prayer, Pope Paul VI said that prayer "depends on the sense of God's presence which we are able to present to our mind either by a natural intuition or by a certain image, or by an act of faith." The Holy Father likened a man conversing with God in prayer to a blind man who realizes that he is in the presence of someone he cannot see. This is a listening posture.

Pope Paul also said that it must be admitted that today's world prays neither willingly nor easily, and he cited two reasons. One he called the "incapacity" to pray, and he ascribed this to a lack of religious training in early life. The other he called a "difficulty" in praying and he ascribed this to either the pride of modern man in his technical prowess, or to the crowd of sensual images stuffed into modern man's brain by mass media. We could overcome much of this "difficulty" by coming to prayer with a genuine listening posture.

In the New Testament there is a theme concerning the "hour" of God's coming. Jesus urges us, "Be constantly on the watch! Stay awake! You do not know when the appointed time will come" (Mark 13:33). Jesus encourages us to "watch and pray" for we do not know when God wishes to reveal Himself to us in moments of prayer.

He speaks to us at the very core of our being and unless we are receptive and open, we may not hear His call.

Should not our constant prayer be, "Lord, teach us to listen."

Chapter Three

Praying Scripturally

"Not on bread alone is man to live but on every utterance that comes from the mouth of God" (Matthew 4:4).

In these days of spiritual renewal there has been a new upsurge of interest in Sacred Scripture. This desire to know God's Word more fully is the work of the Holy Spirit. Many new and popular translations of the Bible have made the reading and praying of His Word easy and enjoyable. Numerous study courses are also helping us to come to a better understanding of the Bible. All these are important and necessary to increase our love and appreciation for the Scriptures.

More important, however, is the fact that the Bible is rapidly becoming the "Prayerbook" for more and more people. The Bible is a spiritual launching pad into a prayerful union with God. This is a new understanding of the Scriptures. In the past, the Bible, for many people, was the symbol of Christianity rather than its source. For others, the Bible was documentary evidence to prove the truths which we believe.

The Holy Spirit is now leading us to appreciate the Word of God, not so much as a treasury of information, but rather as the prime source for our Christian prayer and formation. As we read God's Word, we are not so much concerned about the exegetical significance of a passage of Scripture, but rather our concern is what God is saying to us in His Word.

The Bible must be the very heart of authentic Christian living. There can be no genuine spiritual formation which is not based and rooted in Gospel Spirituality. Through the inspiration of the Holy Spirit we are beginning to realize that God is speaking to us personally through His Word and that He does have a special message for us each day as we come to listen in the very depths of our being.

Approaches to Scripture

We can approach Sacred Scripture in various ways, but not all of them will lead us to a personal encounter with Christ. First we could try to find the exact words of Jesus and the exact circumstances in which He lived and spoke. Time and effort spent in this kind of research will bear little fruit and will be of little use for our prayer life. We really do not have a biography of Jesus as we understand a biography today. Except for the obvious fact that His birth and early life preceded His public life, which, in turn, preceded His death and resurrection, we can find few of the events in the life of Jesus in chronological order. The events in the life of Jesus are thematic and theological rather than chronological. Jesus did not put aside a day when He spoke on prayer and another time when He explained the mercy and compassion of His Father. The Gospel writers group together certain ideas and teachings. For instance, in Luke 15, we find the touching parables on God's mercy. The writers also have collected the instructions of Jesus on prayer and put them together for our better understanding. The Gospels, then, are inspired expressions of faith in the person and saving message of Jesus as the risen Lord and Savior of all people.

The second way of approaching the Scriptures is to inquire as to what the Holy Spirit intended by inspiring the writers of God's Word. What did these authors mean and what was their purpose? This is the concern of Scriptural scholarship and exegesis. Studies in archeology, ancient cultures and literature both preceding and contemporary to biblical times can help us understand much more about the meaning of the books of the Bible. This knowledge can help us grow in the saving knowledge and faith of Jesus. This can also enrich our prayer life, but it will not bring us to a personal encounter with Jesus.

Scholars without faith can make Scripture an object of investigation, but this scientific and critical study can never bring them to the very heart of Scripture, to the point of meeting Christ personally. I know a person who has spent endless hours in research trying to establish whether or not Jesus actually wore a beard. Such a study may satisfy someone's curiosity, but will hardly enrich his prayer life. It has been said that Scripture is a locked house with the key inside. We must live inside. To enter we must be in Christ. We must live in faith.

The third way of approaching Scripture is our principal concern here for our prayer life. The approach is: What is God saying to me personally now as I read or listen to His Word? The style of writing and the literary expression of God's Word has been shaped by the cultures and personalities of the writers, and also by the translators of our times, but God is just as present and alive in Sacred Scripture as He is in the Holy Eucharist. This is the teaching of Vatican II, "The Church has always venerated the Divine Scriptures as she venerates the Body of the Lord, since from the table of both the Word of God and of the Body of Christ, she unceasingly receives and offers to believers the bread of life, especially in the Sacred Liturgy. Just as the life of the Church grows through faithful participation in the Eucharistic mystery, so we hope for a new surge of spiritual life from intensified veneration of God's Word, which lasts forever" *(Dogmatic Constitution on Divine Revelation, par. 21).*

These are two different kinds of presence, but both are real. If I do not believe this, then, God is not present or saving for me in His Word, just as those who do not believe in the real presence of Jesus in the Eucharist cannot be nourished by His Eucharistic presence.

When we listen to God's Word in faith, it can penetrate the deepest areas of our being. God's Word is still the all-powerful force which created and sustains the universe. His Word can recreate, and save all who gratefully listen to that Word in faith. Listening to His Word is a new and exciting dimension in our prayer life which the Holy Spirit is opening up to us.

Present in His Word

Sacred Scripture is not only the Word of God, but Christ Himself is actually present in His Word. From Vatican II we received some powerful insights into the Word of God especially as a dimension for our prayer life. The bishops reminded us of Christ's unique presence in Scripture. In the first document to come out of the Council, we read, "He (Christ) is present in His Word, since it is He Himself who speaks when the Holy Scriptures are read in the Church" *(Constitution on the Sacred Liturgy, par. 7).*

The presence of Jesus among us and in us always has the same purpose. By His presence and what He does, Jesus is always the Redeemer. His redemptive work continues daily in the life of every human being. By His presence Jesus creates a channel of salvation with men.

The presence of Jesus in Scripture is a mysterious presence but a real presence nonetheless. It is different from His Eucharistic presence, but no less real.

We may think of the Bible as a ciborium containing not only the Word of the Lord, but His presence as well. As we receive Jesus sacramentally in Holy Communion, He nourishes and strengthens us. He gives us the spiritual vitality and energy we need for the duties of each day. Even more, His presence with us and within us reassures us that we are not walking the road of life alone, but He is our constant companion. Every time we receive Him in the Eucharistic banquet, He shares once again His divine life with us.

As we pray His Word each day, Jesus personally comes to us to renew and implement His presence within us. Our prayer time each day is like a host from the ciborium of His Word. His presence in His Word brings us new life and hope, new energy and encouragement. As we eat at the table of His Word our lives are deeply nourished and enriched.

God invites us to the banquet of His Word, "Come to me heedfully, listen that you may have life . . . So shall my word be, that goes forth from my mouth; it shall not return to me void, but shall do my will, achieving the end for which I sent it"

(Isaiah 55:3, 11).

The Church has admirably blended these two great sources of spiritual growth in the Liturgy of the Word and the Liturgy of the Eucharist in the Holy Sacrifice of the Mass. Each day we are nurtured by His Word and nourished by His sacramental presence. Such is the loving providence of our Father!

As Vatican II's *Dogmatic Constitution on Divine Revelation* points out, "In the Sacred Books, the Father Who is in heaven meets His children with great love and speaks with them; and the force and power in the Word of God is so great that it remains the support and energy of the Church, the strength of faith for her sons, the food of the soul, the pure and perennial source of spiritual life . . . " *(par. 21)*.

Praying with Sacred Scripture establishes a communion of thought between two people who love each other, who share together and who enjoy being together. Jesus is first of these two persons and each one of us is the other person when we are alone with Him in His Word.

When we read or pray God's Word with faith, Jesus Himself speaks to us. Even though the Holy Spirit inspired the authors of the Sacred Books to write centuries ago, the Words of God are for today. Jesus is speaking them to you and to me *today*, at this very hour.

The redeeming action of Christ knows no time, but goes on daily. It is for all men of all times, even for the ages yet unborn. Jesus speaks to His Church in eternity. As we read and listen to Christ's Word with faith, we are hearing Jesus speak them to us now.

Scripture is an everlasting word, always being said. It is being spoken for us today. In the *Epistle to the Hebrews* all the quotations are in the present

39

tense. In other words, they are being spoken to us today. "Wherefore, as the Holy Spirit *says:* 'Today, if you should hear his voice, harden not your hearts . . . ' *(Hebrews 3:7);* and, also, in that same letter, "The Holy Spirit *attests* this to us, for after saying, 'This is the covenant I will make with them after those days, says the Lord: I will put my laws in their hearts and I will write them on their minds,' He also says, 'Their sins and their transgressions I will remember no more' " *(Hebrews 10:15-17).*

As we pray with His Word and are puzzled about some word or truth, Jesus can communicate the meaning of His words directly to our minds. This is not the case in reading a human author. If we read a book, we can comprehend only what our human intelligence can grasp. The author's thought comes to us indirectly through signs and words which we must interpret. On the other hand, when we hear the words of Scripture, Jesus can and does communicate the understanding of the truth they express. He arouses in us the same sentiments which are His. This helps us "to put on the mind of Christ." This is what St. Paul meant when he wrote, "Let the word of Christ, rich as it is, dwell in you" *(Colossians 3:16).*

Mary of Bethany must have experienced this intimate union of mind and heart as she sat at His feet and let His every word find a home in her heart. Jesus could say of her, "Mary has chosen the better portion and she shall not be deprived of it" *(Luke 10:38-42).* The disciples on the road to Emmaus had a similar indepth experience. They tried to express it in these words, "Were not our hearts burning inside us as he talked to us on the road and explained the Scriptures to us?" *(Luke 24:32).*

40

Faith

God invites us to come to the table of His Word. He permits us to "taste the good word of God" *(Hebrews 6:5).* But at times we are so slow to appreciate its savor. As we are able to spend time enjoying the bread from His table of the Word, it becomes more enjoyable each day. There is an ever-increasing hunger for this delectable food, if our hearts are disposed to receive His Word. The disposition which is required is faith.

We must have ears to hear the Word of God and the ears are not the ears of the body. We must hear His Word deep inside, "Let him who has ears heed the Spirit's Word to the churches!" *(Revelation 2:7).* We must listen with the ears of faith. It is faith which opens the Word of God to us, "That is why we thank God constantly that in receiving his message from us you took it, not as the word of men, but as it truly is, the word of God at work within you who believe" *(I Thessalonians 2:13).* Jesus implied that it would take faith to understand the Word. After telling the parable of the Sower, He said: "Let everyone who has ears attend to what he has heard" *(Luke 8:8).*

Like every spiritual reality given to us during our earthly sojourn, Scripture has two facets: one apparent to the senses; the other visible only to eyes of faith. It was so with Jesus. His enemies saw Him with their eyes and they nailed Him to a cross. Those who believed in Him, adored Him as their God. This is also true of the Church whose human side can be seen by all, but whose mystery is hidden from many. We can say the same about the Holy Eucharist. To some the Eucharist is simply bread, and to others it is really, truly and substantially the body of the glorified Jesus.

Jesus explained this absolute necessity of faith

41

in such picturesque terms. "The sheep hear his voice as he calls his own by name and leads them out. When he has brought out (all) those that are his, he walks in front of them, and the sheep follow him because they recognize his voice" *(John 10:3-4)*. Those without faith may hear the words, but only the sheep with faith will hear His voice. The voice discloses the person. Words express ideas, but the voice reveals the person. The Words of Scripture can be compared with ordinary human words, but the voice behind those words brings us into contact with the Person. Only faith has ears to hear the voice. Faith alone establishes contact with Jesus. Each sheep is called by name. The encounter is personal and becomes a dialogue. On Easter morning, Jesus merely called a person by name, "Mary." Instantly, Mary recognized that voice and answered, "Rabbouni!" *(John 20:11-18)*. Thus it will be for us. As we come to listen intently with the ears of faith to His Word, we soon will hear not words, but His voice.

The person who does not hear the voice, sees in the Bible only the dead letter. His vision is myopic and bound. The person who comes with faith and with uncovered eyes has only to open to Scripture to come face to face with the Lord in glory. He feels himself transformed. As Paul puts it, "All of us, gazing on the Lord's glory with unveiled faces, are being transformed from glory to glory into his very image by the Lord who is the Spirit" *(II Corinthians 3:18)*.

Methodology

For most of us, using Sacred Scripture as prayer opens up a whole new concept in our prayer life which promises to be a rewarding experience. How do we begin to pray with God's Word? **Prayer is** primarily listening. When we pray with Scripture we are listening to what God is saying to us through His Word. Prayer is an aloneness with God. In the solitude of our hearts we rivet our attention on Him and listen with our whole being.

In preparing to pray with God's Word, it is beneficial to follow a definite procedure. In the first place we pick a short passage of Scripture which we wish to use for our prayer, (e.g., parable of the vine and the branches, *John 15:1-8).* Choosing a text ahead of time allows for some long-range preparation. If we are going to pray in the morning, let us say, it is well to select a passage the evening before, read it slowly, and quietly let some thought linger and soak in. This remote preparation has already created in us a receptive mood before we actually begin our prayer the next morning. If we are unable to prepare for our prayer so far in advance, it is well to make the selection of a passage before we proceed with the other recommended steps in our preparation.

Second, a time for prayer is important. Having a regular time set aside for prayer helps us to enter into the spirit of prayer a little easier. Many people find the morning a particularly suitable time for prayer. At this time of the day we are usually more relaxed than later in the day. If we choose a time during the day, the transition from a busy work-a-day world into prayer is not so readily achieved for most of us. Each person must choose the time which is best for him, but a regularly scheduled time seems to be a "must" for most people.

The third step in the preparation procedure is the place for our prayer. A definite place for prayer is essential, be it our den, bedroom, favorite chair or even a special prayer room. A designated place for listening to God puts us into a prayerful mood even as we approach the spot.

Some people have a little prayer corner all set up. Here we may enthrone the Bible with a candle. Here also we may place a particular pebble, a letter, a gift or any object which has spoken to us of God. As we learn to listen, it is surprising to discover how many ways and means God uses to communicate Himself to us. Loving Father that He is, He will use any and every media to reach His children.

Fourth, settle into a comfortable posture, conducive to peacefully listening to God. A comfortable, relaxed posture is imperative for prayer. Take a few moments to relax and quiet yourself. Relax your limbs and face muscles. Place all your cares and concerns in the Lord's hands and let Him take care of them while you spend your time in prayer with Him. Resolve to give Him this time and do not permit anything to interfere. This is your special date with the Lord. It might even be well to take the phone off the hook.

Before taking up a Scriptural passage as the basis for our prayer, it is advisable to spend some time in becoming aware of God's loving presence with us and within us. This is the fifth step in our procedure.

Concentrating on our breathing is not only a good way to relax, but it is also one way to recall God's abiding presence. As we breathe, we may think of inhaling not only oxygen, but also inhaling His divine life. Be aware that God fills us with His presence, that He loves us unconditionally, that He is always conscious of us and always with us. Furthermore, as we inhale and exhale we can quietly utter the name of Jesus with our hearts and not only with our lips. Pronouncing His name with our lips may interrupt the progress of resting totally relaxed in the arms of the Lord.

We should reflect on the many different ways in

which Christ is incarnated in our world and on His closeness to us, especially in His Word. He is Emmanuel — God-with-us. We come to prayer, then, with an expectant faith that God will use His "Living Word" to speak directly to us and that His message will be pertinent for us at this precise moment in time.

Finally, pray! Slowly read the Scriptural passage. Believe that the words are God's own words and are meant for us — here and now. Pray by simply listening to what God is saying to us. Rest on a word, a phrase, a verse. Linger on a resting place. Savor it. Repeat the words. Reflect on the words in silence. Quietly listen. Soak in God's presence, feel the warmth of His love, taste His sweetness. Stay with the same passage during the whole prayer period and repeat it as often as you like.

Some time ago, I had a miserable, frustrating, exhausting day. Nothing went according to plan — *my* plan. That evening as I prayed Psalm 34, the Lord really spoke to me in verse six. The psalmist struck at the very heart of my problem that day when he said: "Look to Him, that you may be radiant with joy." That was my resting place. That message hit home. All day long I was looking at myself, *my* schedule, *my* plans, *my* will. In my frustration, I failed to look at Him. The Lord really refocused my attention that evening. This is just one incident showing how the Lord speaks.

On another occasion I was using a verse from Scripture that I had previously used dozens of times. Jesus spoke to my heart when He reminded me, "As the Father has loved me, so I have loved you" *(John 15:9)*. The overwhelming thought of the Father's infinite love for His Son is exactly the same love with which Jesus loves me. Words cannot express the experience which I enjoyed at this

45

special message for me.

A sister, who was making an individually directed retreat and also using Scripture as the basis of her prayer, said, "After two days of listening to God telling me that He loves me, I have come two million light years closer to Jesus. Now I love Him in a much deeper way and I know that He loves me."

A whole host of directives might be given to guide us in our scriptural praying. Here is a summary of some pertinent guidelines which were given by an experienced retreat director.

Be there with Jesus and *for* Him! Yes, be there. Have you ever talked with someone who was with you bodily, but not present to you with attention and heart? We know how frustrating this experience can be. Jesus deserves the best — our full attention.

Really *want* Jesus! Hunger for Him. Prepare for His coming and for His Word, as you would eagerly prepare for a visit with the dearest person in your life. Invite Jesus to reveal and communicate Himself to you, to speak to you and teach you how to listen deeply to Him.

Listen to Jesus! Listen with faith. Listen deeply and reverently. Listen with trust. Listen with hunger to be fed by His Word. Listen with gratitude and in peace. Listen without searching for hidden meanings in His Word. Be simple as a child nestled in his father's lap; peacefully listen to His story.

Let Jesus! Respond in any way you want to, or feel moved to respond. Be genuinely yourself and respond honestly, freely, spontaneously, reverently. Speak what is in your heart, say what you feel, even when you feel like complaining. Remember that when you don't know what to say, the Holy Spirit prays in you and for you. Just speaking or whispering the name of Jesus rhythmically with your breathing, or repeating words of praise and thanks are profoundly prayerful responses.

Contemplative prayer is more feeling, listening to, and being aware of God, our loving Father, and of Jesus, our Brother, and of the Holy Spirit living in us, rather than saying or doing anything. It is consciously being with Him and letting Him be for us the loving God that He is, letting Him fill us with His Spirit and letting Jesus become more and more alive and real to us.

With Samuel let our constant prayer be, "Speak, Lord, for your servant is listening" *(I Samuel 3:9).*

Chapter Four

Fruits Of Scriptural Praying

"My Father has been gloried in your bearing much fruit and becoming my disciples" (John 15:8).

In this age of the Holy Spirit, we are being called to a deep spiritual renewal. God's infinite wisdom is so apparent in the method which He is using to accomplish this renewal within us. Through the power of His Spirit, He is drawing us gently but firmly to the treasury of Sacred Scripture as the fountain of our prayer. The Spirit is creating within us a longing and even a yearning for His Word. According to St. Paul, only God can instill this desire in us. "It is God who, in his good will toward you, begets in you any measure of desire or achievement" *(Philippians 2:13)*.

God not only begets this desire for genuine spiritual renewal in our hearts, but He is also stirring the embers of this desire into a consuming hunger and thirst for His Word. He is doing so because there is no other single tool more effective in accomplishing a spiritual renewal within each one of us. Let us consider some of the fruits which praying with Scripture produces in our lives.

Knowing God

The fruits of praying with Scripture are far too many to enumerate and too personal to attempt to evaluate. The first choice fruit of Scriptural praying is the fact that we get to know God. It is only as we listen to God speaking to us that we really come to know Him. It may seem paradoxical to say that we can know very much about God without really knowing Him. There is a great difference in knowing about a person and in knowing him.

By way of example, I could give you a whole host of facts about a friend of mine, but you still do not know him. You only know *about* him. However, if you meet this friend of mine and converse with him for some time, then you will begin to know him. The more you listen to him, the better you will know him.

It is hardly possible to know a person well until we have listened to him speak. By his speech he reveals very much about himself, his hopes and ambitions, his joys and sorrows, his likes and dislikes. In brief, if we listen intently, we will not merely hear his words, we will really come to know him.

The same is true of our relationship with God. Intellectually we may know much about God — that He is omniscient, omnipresent, omnipotent, immutable, eternal. This is knowledge about God without really knowing Him as a loving, personal Father. We can best know God as He reveals Himself to us through His Word. St. Jerome puts it rather bluntly: "Ignorance of the Scripture is ignorance of Christ." Yes, God does reveal much about Himself as we listen to His Word. It is also true that the more intently we listen to God, the better will we come to know Him. We can love a person only after we know him.

What does God tell us about Himself? He discloses through His Word that He is a God of might and power. God spoke and the universe came into being. The psalmist sings of the majesty of God and the dignity He gave to man.

"When I behold your heavens, the work of your fingers, the moon and the stars which you set in place — what is man that you should be mindful of him, or the son of man that you should care for him? You have made him a little less than the angels, and crowned him with glory and honor" (Psalm 8:4-6).

God tells us, furthermore, that He is an all-loving and an all-knowing God. He is concerned about us at every moment of the day. He knows when we stand and when we sit. He knows every thought before it comes into our mind and every word before it is on our lips (Psalm 139).

God Loves Me

As we pray certain passages from the Old Testament, we become more and more aware how much God really does love us. We need to know that God loves us. We need assurance that we are lovable. This is important because many of us do not love ourselves. We know ourselves deep down inside. We are aware of our weaknesses, our selfishness, our failures, our sinfulness. Knowing ourselves, we wonder how God could really love us.

Furthermore, it will not affect our lives too significantly to have others tell us how much God really does love us. It is more important to hear God speak to us and tell us Himself how very much He loves us.

God not only tells us, but He proves to us that He really does love us. He says to us personally, "With age-old love I have loved you" (Jeremiah

31:3). Listen to what He is saying to us through the great Prophet Isaiah, "Fear not, for I have redeemed you; I have called you by name: you are mine"; "You are precious in my eyes and glorious, and because I love you"; and, again, "It is I, I, who wipe out, for my own sake, your offenses; your sins I remember no more." All this in one chapter *(Isaiah 43:1 & 4 & 25)*. In another place our loving Father asks a rhetorical question, "Can a mother forget her infant, be without tenderness for the child of her womb? Even should she forget, I will never forget you. See, upon the palms of my hands I have written your name" *(Isaiah 49:15-16)*. Old Testament passages which tell us of God's personal love for each one of us could be multiplied over and over again.

As we pray with Sacred Scripture, we become more and more convinced of God's overwhelming love. Even if our motives are often self-centered, God says, "I love you." In spite of our sinfulness, God still says, "I love you no matter what you've done." Regardless of our failure to reach the plateau of perfection that we have set for ourselves, God continues to love us "with an everlasting love."

Jesus gives us a portrait of our heavenly Father as a loving, merciful, compassionate God in that touching parable of the Prodigal Son *(Luke 15:11-32)*. Already before Jesus came to tell us of His Father and ours, God spoke to us and told us something about Himself through the Prophet Hosea, "I drew them with human cords, with bands of love. I fostered them like one who raises an infant to his cheeks" *(Hosea 11:4)*.

God tells us more about His unbounded love for us as He pleads with us in the Liturgy of Good Friday. "My people, what have I done to you? How have I offended you? Answer me. What more

51

could I have done for you and have not done it?" These plaintive words, addressed to us by our loving Father through His prophet, reveal the depths of His love for us regardless of our response to that love.

A basic step to prayer is this conviction that God loves us with an infinite love and nothing we do can change that love. We must come to know Him as a loving, compassionate, forgiving Father who welcomes His errant children with open arms.

When we are convinced that we are loved, only then can we be open and honest with ourselves and with others. There is no reason for pretense or sham. When we know that we are accepted, we need not wear any masks, or do any playacting. We can live in freedom and sincerity.

A consciousness of God's great love for us can lead us into greater depths of prayer. Deeply aware of His loving presence we want to whisper in the quiet of our hearts, "I love You, too"; or, "Thank You, Father, for loving me, for Your abiding presence sanctifying me at every moment of the day."

No Greater Love

In the New Testament, Jesus tells us frequently how much He loves each one of us. He says, "As the Father has loved me, so I have loved you" (John 15:9). Reflect for a moment on what Jesus is really saying about His love for us. The Father's love for Jesus is absolutely limitless. Jesus is assuring us that His love for us is infinite because it is as great as the Father's love for Him. Furthermore, the Holy Trinity is a community of perfect love; consequently, the Holy Spirit loves us with an infinite love. How incomprehensible, how astounding is God's love for us!

At another time Jesus explained, "There is no

greater love than this: to lay down one's life for one's friends" *(John 15:13)*. The very next day Jesus proved His love for us by laying down His life for us. The Holy Spirit speaking to us through Paul gives us another reassurance of the love which Jesus had for us. "Christ died for us godless men. It is rare that anyone should lay down his life for a just man, though it is barely possible that for a good man someone may have the courage to die. It is precisely in that that God proves his love for us" *(Romans 5:6-7)*.

In addition to telling us of His great love for us, Jesus demonstrated by His whole life and all that He did, how much He loves us. He reached out in love to the wedding party of Cana and worked His first miracle. He hugged the leper *(Luke 5:13)*. The sinful woman heard Him say, "Your sins are forgiven" *(Luke 7:48)*. And why — because of her great love. The Samaritan woman felt His loving acceptance of her in spite of her sinfulness and she became an apostle of love for her own people *(John 4)*.

The whole healing mission of Jesus gave evidence of His infinite love, " . . . the blind recover their sight, cripples walk, lepers are cured, the deaf hear, dead men are raised to life, and the poor have the good news preached to them" *(Matthew 11:5)*.

Even His enemies felt the warmth of His redeeming love, "Father, forgive them; they do not know what they are doing" *(Luke 23:34)*.

This kind of love is overwhelming. It is beyond our human comprehension. As we strive to fathom its immensity we become more and more aware of the gravity of our infidelities. We see them as a rejection of God's love for us. Sin is saying "no" to love. However, there is no reason for us to lose hope. Love surmounts all our failure.

As we spend time in prayer each day, listening

to God speaking to us through His Word, the conviction that He does really love us becomes firm. This conviction affects our whole life. We are happy to accept ourselves as we are. We find it much easier to accept others as they are. We will find great peace in our lives simply because we know at the very core of our being that we are known and loved by God.

Spiritual Energy

Praying with Sacred Scripture is a great source of vitality to us on our daily journey to Emmaus. The routine of life becomes monotonous and sometimes even discouraging. On our pilgrimage to the Father the road is often rough and rocky. At times the hills seem high and the valleys quite deep. How often we need to be reassured and encouraged! God's Word is a limitless fountain of inspiration, hope and encouragement as we trek along the road of life.

Here is just one instance of St. Paul telling us how valuable is God's Word during these days of our earthly exile, "Everything written before our time was written for our instruction, that we might derive hope from the lessons of patience and the words of encouragement in the Scriptures" *(Romans 15:4).*

Life is plagued with so much decision-making. It is difficult to ascertain just what God wants of us in certain situations. Again, there is no magic formula, but we can be assured that God does give us direction if we listen to Him each day as He speaks to us through His Word.

Again it is St. Paul who assures us that many of our needs will be met in God's Word. He writes, "All Scripture is inspired of God and is useful for teaching — for reproof, correction, and training in holiness so that the man of God may be fully competent and equipped for every good work" *(II Timothy 3:16)*. As we pray passages like this one, we find great reassurance for our daily living.

A quiet time of listening is so essential to our spiritual growth. As we listen, God assures us that He is aware of our every anxiety and worry. He knows full well the problems which perplex us. In His Sermon on the Mount, Jesus instructs us, "Your heavenly Father knows all that you need. Seek first his Kingship over you, his way of holiness, and all these things will be given you besides" *(Matthew 6:32-33)*. We seek His Kingdom as we listen to His Word.

Purification

A great change takes place within us as we pray with Sacred Scripture. It has a purifying effect upon us. As we ponder what God is saying, we soon perceive whether or not our mind is the same as Christ's mind. We discover whether or not we are seeing things through Jesus' eyes.

As we expose our thinking to His Word, a real cleansing process takes place within us. We see how much of our thinking might be pure rationalization. If our attitudes are foreign to the mind of Christ, we become more and more aware of this dichotomy as we pray. Perhaps we have been rather self-centered and myopic in our outlook. As we are purified by His Word, our self-centeredness begins to fade and our vision takes on the cosmic vision of Christ.

As we faithfully pray each day, a whole "metanoia" is under way within our being. Jesus alerted us to this conversion when He told us through His apostles, "You are clean already, thanks to the word I have spoken to you" *(John 15:3)*.

God's Word is a powerful Word. By His Word, the universe came into being. His Word has the power to change bread and wine into His body and blood. Through the power of His Word, the blind see, the lame walk and the dead are raised to life again. His Word not only cleanses us of our sins, but also has the power to heal us of our resentments, our impatience, our selfishness and the whole host of other weaknesses which lead us away from God.

St. Paul did not mince words in telling us how effective God's Word can be in our purification. "Indeed, God's Word is living and effective, sharper than any two-edged sword. It penetrates and divides soul and spirit, joints and marrow; it judges the reflections and thoughts of the heart. Nothing is concealed from him; all lies bare and exposed to the eyes of him to whom we must render an account" *(Hebrews 4:12-14)*.

A daily prayer time with Scripture is an effective way for us to permit the Holy Spirit to mold us into a person radiating and reflecting Christ. With St. Paul, we, too, can say, "The life I live now is not my own: Christ is living in me" *(Galatians 2:20)*.

Transformation

The power of God's Word can effect within us a complete transformation. As we feed at the table of His Word, we will discover a change coming over us. Our thinking, our attitudes, our relationship to others will gradually change. We may not even perceive the transformation taking place within us, but His Word is powerful and effective.

Daily, we eat food to sustain our physical life. After we have enjoyed a good meal, we are not particularly aware of the food we have eaten. However, the food is being digested and assimilated, carrying strength to every part of our body. Nourishing food keeps our body healthy and vigorous.

Similarly, praying with Scripture matures us spiritually. St. Paul is quite imperative when he advises us, "You must lay aside your former way of life and the old self which deteriorates through illusion and desire, and acquire a fresh, spiritual way of thinking. You must put on the new man created in God's image, whose justice and holiness are born of truth" *(Ephesians 4:22-24)*. And furthermore, "Do not conform yourselves to this age but be transformed by the renewal of your mind, so that you may judge what is God's will, what is good and pleasing and perfect" *(Romans 12:2)*.

The Christian who wants to follow Christ more closely, who wants to reflect the peace and joy of the Lord in his interpersonal relations, must come frequently, even daily, to the table of the Lord's Word to be filled and formed into a new man. Nowhere can we discover the mind of Christ more clearly than in His own Word.

Just as we take food several times a day rather than one huge consumption every few days, so with God's Word we need to come daily to listen to what He is telling us.

At times we may pray with Scripture and nothing seems to happen. We have no new insights, no great spiritual experiences, no real sense of His presence. We may be disappointed and even frustrated. On the other hand, how can we be sure that nothing is happening? An indepth transformation may be under way without our awareness of what is taking place within us. Perhaps a little example may illustrate the point. I may sit down and enjoy a delicious meal. I may savor and enjoy every morsel of food. It could be a delightful experience. On another occasion I may not be feeling well, or the food just does not appeal to my fancy; hence I eat with little relish. Yet both meals may well be equally nutritious. The same can be true of our time spent in prayer. On one day our prayer might be a real experience of God's presence. On another day, our prayer might be dry and dull, but who are we to say which is the more pleasing prayer in God's sight?

Jesus says to us, "If you live in me, and my Words stay part of you, you may ask what you will — it will be done for you" *(John 15:7)*.

Joy

The whole Christian era was inaugurated on a note of joy. When the angels announced to the shepherds that Jesus was born in Bethlehem, they underscored what effects this should have on the world. "I come to proclaim good news to you — tidings of great joy to be shared by the whole people" *(Luke 2:10)*. Even today our materialistic world pauses each year to be joyous during the Christmas season.

Jesus Himself informs us of the effect His Word should have upon us. As we pray Sacred Scripture we shall experience a real interior joy unlike any joy we may have previously experienced. Jesus is the Word. He came to reveal the message of the Father. This is the Good News and this is the source of our joy. Jesus also told us the reason for His teaching, "All this I tell you that my joy may be yours and your joy may be complete" *(John 15:11)*.

Later on, the beloved Apostle John explained what and why he is writing. "What we have seen and heard we proclaim in turn to you so that you may share life . . . Indeed, our purpose in writing you this, is that our joy may be complete" *(I John*

1:3-4).

St. Paul singled out joy as a special fruit of the Holy Spirit. "In contrast, the fruit of the Spirit is love, joy, peace . . . " *(Galatians 5:22).*

Paul also explains what our Christian life is all about: "The Kingdom of God is not a matter of eating and drinking, but of justice, peace, and the joy that is given by the Holy Spirit" *(Romans 14:17).*

As we pray with Scripture, we, too, will experience the joy which the Good News can bring us. Filled with His joy, we can become apostles of joy to all those who traverse our path each day.

These fruits, which we singled out, are only a few of the many which will be produced in us as we assiduously pray with Scripture each day. These few have been dealt with to encourage us and to convince us of the transformation which will assuredly take place within us. God's Word is a mighty Word and who of us can estimate its power?

God Himself tells us how effective His Word is in our lives.

"For just as from the heavens the rain and snow come down and do not return there till they have watered the earth, making it fertile and fruitful, giving seed to him who sows, and bread to him who eats, so shall my word be that goes forth from my mouth; it shall not return to me void, but shall do my will, achieving the end for which I sent it" *(Isaiah 55:10-11).*

Chapter Five

Praying Meditatively

"I remember the deeds of the Lord; yes, I remember your wonders of old. And I meditate on your works; your exploits I ponder" (Psalm 77:12-13).

We are pilgrim people. We belong to a pilgrim Church. Our pilgrimage is leading us back to the Father. As we journey along we need rest and relaxation, refueling and refreshing. We have all made journeys taking us away from home for a longer or shorter distance and are well aware of the necessities required for these journeys. Along the highways we find park-like rest stops with tables and benches for our comfort and convenience, for our rest and relaxation. Along the roadways there are many people who are prepared to supply us with the necessary fuel and other supplies for our vehicle of travel. Others are ready to serve us the food and drink for our physical well-being. Our blessings are many.

On our pilgrimage to the Father, all of our spiritual needs have been more than adequately supplied by a loving, provident God. We need to know that our Father is with us as we journey along. We travel with greater peace and confidence knowing that all our needs are generously provided. We need this assurance in order to persevere on our pilgrimage. At times the valleys along life's highway may seem very deep and impenetrable. The mountains may seem high and difficult to climb. Along the way we need hope and encouragement, reassurance and refreshment.

All this comes to us as we spend time in meditative prayer. Meditation is our rest stop, our refueling and refreshing oasis. Meditation is that form of prayer which centers in the mind. When we meditate we think about God, and all His wonderful works. We picture, ponder and reflect on God, our Father, or Jesus, our Redeemer, or the Holy Spirit, our Sanctifier. Our mind seeks understanding and insight. In meditation our lips are quiet but our mind is active. In meditation we strive to raise our minds and hearts to God in silence in order to offer Him our worship, adoration, thanks and petitions.

The royal troubadour of the Lord in one of His Psalms gives us not only the purpose, but also the importance of meditation. David had an ardent longing for God and thus he prayed,

"O God, you are my God whom I seek; for you my flesh pines and my soul thirsts like the earth, parched, lifeless and without water. Thus have I gazed toward you in the sanctuary to see your power and your glory. For your kindness is a greater good than life; my lips shall glorify you. Thus will I bless you while I live; lifting up my hands, I will call upon your name. As with the riches of a banquet shall my soul be satisfied, and with exultant lips my mouth shall praise you. I will remember you upon my couch, and through the night-watches I will meditate on you" *(Psalm 63:1-9)*.

The psalmist not only showed us all the ele-

61

ments of meditative prayer, but this is a meditation in itself.

When we desire to know God better, we will start reverently and reflectively to ponder His majesty and goodness. We can begin by pondering word by word a prayer, such as the Our Father or a psalm. We may also take a scene from the Gospel and reflect upon its meaning and the lesson it teaches us. Again we can reflect on our attitude to life, be it our patience or lack of it, our readiness to be of service to others, our relationship to others, our response to God, etc.

We bring one of these subjects of meditation to God and we speak to Him about it. As we bring it to God we discover new insights, and encouragement. This kind of prayer we call meditation.

If we spend time in meditation faithfully, or if we can honestly say that we have tried to do so, we will come to a moment when we recognize our own poverty and our inability even to pray. Then we come in loving trust to God and abandon ourselves totally into His hands.

We can expect to encounter some difficulties as we spend time in meditative prayer. We may try to concentrate and respond in loving prayer with little or no success. However, the desire to pray still lingers with us. Our hearts yearn to be with God and be attentive to the divine depths of His being, but we encounter only dryness, or even a distaste for prayer or bewilderment. Nevertheless, something in us still wants to remain at prayer. We feel strongly that we are really not doing anything ourselves, but something is happening within us. Then comes a great peace. We know that only God can bring us to prayer. All this is gift. All this comes from God. This realization, too, is the fruit of meditation.

Meditative Reading

One type of mental prayer is called meditative reading or reflective reading. This is a simple form of prayer and fits our many moods.

We will profit much more from our prayer if we prepare for it by reading the Word of God regularly. It is to be expected that prayer will be difficult if we put no spiritual thoughts into our minds. Meditative reading is an excellent way of filling our mind with thoughts about God and His loving concern for each one of us.

Methodology

In this type of prayer we read a bit of the Word of God, we think about what we have read; then we speak to God of whatever comes to our minds. Perhaps the best way of explaining meditative reading is by briefly outlining such a process. Let us select a passage from St. Luke (24:13-35), relating the story of the disciples on the road to Emmaus. Read the passage slowly and pensively. Pause and rest on a certain word, a phrase, or a sentence which speaks to you. Think about the import of the words, then speak to Jesus about them.

Here is a little sample of the procedure which can be followed. We offer this example with the understanding that we are using only a few phrases chosen at random. Other verses also lend themselves easily to prayer. In fact, they may speak more eloquently to you than those we have selected. Together let us reflect on some thoughts from the account of Jesus meeting Cleopas and his companion as they journeyed toward Emmaus.

Verse 17, "They were restrained from recognizing him ... " Yes, these two disciples were so absorbed in their own problem that they were not concerned about the stranger who joined them. Jesus is such a gentle God. He does not force His presence upon them; He just joined them as they journeyed along. Jesus was sensitive to the anguish which these disciples were experiencing.

Jesus, I become so absorbed in the mundane and the temporalities of everyday living that I am not really open to what You are saying to me through others. I am not really listening. Please help me to get my focus off myself and keep it on You.

Thank You for accompanying me on my daily trek to Emmaus. Help me to respond to Your presence.

Verse 25, "How slow you are to believe all that the prophets have announced!" The vision of the disciples was so myopic. They were so absorbed in their own grief and disappointment. They saw all their hopes for a restoration of the kingdom come tumbling down when Jesus was not only rejected by His own people but assassinated as a common criminal. They were really not looking at these events through God's eyes. They had little faith and trust in what Jesus had taught them — that it was good for them that He suffer and die. There is a great mystery here in the death of Jesus, but the disciples could not fully grasp God's plan of salvation.

Jesus, how narrow is my horizon! I am concerned only with my own will. I want everything to happen according to my expectations. I seldom really come and ask what You want of me. My faith, too, under trial is weak. How often I question Your will! How often I ask why this should happen to me!

Verse 29, "Stay with us. It is nearly evening — the day is practically over." Finally, the disciples began to show concern for the stranger who joined them. They were anxious about Him as He had no place to stay. He had not yet eaten and must be hungry after His journey with them. Their loving concern for Him, and their invitation to Him to remain with them, was the moment for Jesus to reach out in love to them.

Jesus, You are a gentle God. You respect my free will. You do not force Yourself upon me. You patiently wait for my invitation. How long You must wait! How thoughtless I am! I try everything else, then finally I turn to You. It is You I should turn to first of all. Jesus, at this very moment, I do invite You once again into my life. Stay with me, always!

Verse 31, "With that their eyes were opened and they recognized him." The disciples recognized Jesus in the breaking of the bread. The Holy Eucharist is such a powerful sign to us of His presence among us. Jesus, help me to recognize You "in the breaking of the bread" and also in every person and situation of my daily living.

Verse 32, "Were not our hearts burning inside us as he talked to us on the road and explained the Scriptures to us." The Word of God is a powerful word. It captivated the hearts of these disciples. It clarified for them the mystery of God's plan of redemption. It gave reason for "the things that went on there (Jerusalem) the last few days." God's Word revealed His great love for them and all mankind.

Jesus, teach me to love, taste and savor Your Word. Your Word can and does change my whole life. Teach me how to listen to Your Word. Thank You for putting the desire to come to Your Word into my heart. Help me to pray Your Word each day.

Verse 33, "They got up immediately and returned to Jerusalem." The disciples were much concerned about their community. Even though they had just made the journey from Jerusalem, they hurried back to share the Good News that Jesus is alive. They were apostles of joy.

Lord, Jesus, You are much alive today, abiding with us and dwelling within us through the power of Your Spirit. You are sharing Your divine life with us that we, too, can become apostles of the Good News to others. Your Resurrection is our hope and our joy. Help us to bring the joy of Your Resurrection to all we meet. We must be Your personification in the world in which we move. Fill us anew with Your divine life that we may be channels of Your love, peace and joy to all who come across our path.

These few, brief reflections are but a little sampling of how to pray meditatively. Each verse, in fact almost every word, of Sacred Scripture is replete with meaning. As we ponder His Word, our lives will gradually be changed. We will see things through His eyes; our attitude will be the same as His! Our mind will gradually become the mind of Christ.

Our life will change. Each day there will be new joys. Visible creation will really become the mirror of God's love. Each person we meet will become brother and sister to us.

Meditation

We will never learn to meditate unless we begin to pray meditatively. Let us review the procedure in making a meditation, realizing that this is only one of several methods.

We begin with a preparatory prayer asking God to help us with our prayer. Beg Him to direct all our thoughts toward Him and to send His Holy Spirit to pray with us and within us. "The Spirit, too, helps us in our weakness for we do not know how to pray as we ought" *(Romans 8:26)*.

Secondly, choose the subject of our meditation. The subject of this suggested outline of a meditation will be the scene of Zacchaeus meeting Jesus. As we read this passage slowly and reflectively, let us put ourselves into the scene. Do not think about it as something which happened centuries ago in a distant land, but rather walk with Jesus, hear His words, accompany Him to the home of Zacchaeus, sit comfortably close to Jesus as He speaks to Zacchaeus. Relive this scene as we read the account of Luke 19:1-10.

"Entering Jericho, he passed through the city. There was a man there named Zacchaeus, the chief tax collector and a wealthy man. He was trying to see what Jesus was like, but being small of stature, was unable to do so because of the crowd. He first ran on in front, then climbed a sycamore tree which was along Jesus' route, in order to see him. When Jesus came to the spot he looked up and said, 'Zacchaeus, hurry down. I mean to stay at your house today.' He quickly descended, and welcomed him with delight. When this was observed, everyone began to murmur, 'He has gone to a sinner's house as a guest.' Zacchaeus stood his ground and said to the Lord: 'I give half my belongings, Lord, to the poor. If I have defrauded anyone in the least, I pay him back fourfold.' Jesus said to him: 'Today salvation has come to this house, for this is what it means to be a son of Abraham. The Son of Man has come to search out and save what was lost.' "

We pause now before going into the meditation to ask God for what we want from this meditation: for example, I may wish to draw closer to Jesus as Zacchaeus did; I may want a deeper conversion experience, or I may wish to be moved to a greater love of Jesus when I realize His merciful and healing love is reaching out to me.

The meditation may be divided into several parts if we wish and the ends we seek may be more than one. Our thoughts may focus on various aspects of the subject under consideration. For example:

A. Zacchaeus had a real desire to see Jesus. He had heard about Him and especially about His loving concern for sinners and tax collectors. Zacchaeus felt himself drawn to Jesus. He probably did not hope to be able to speak with Him, but he did hope, at least, to see Jesus. He never anticipated the loving-kindness Jesus extended to him. Watch Zacchaeus as he climbs the tree. His desire to see Jesus was so great that he cared little about what people might think of him climbing into the tree. He was willing to go to any length to see Jesus, hence he used his ingenuity.

As we reflect on this scene and try to experience what Zacchaeus experienced in his heart, and also strive to experience the love of Jesus for sinners including ourselves, we ask ourselves what efforts are we making to draw closer to Jesus? We can dwell on this thought for considerable time. Be alone with Jesus now. Ask Him to give us some pointers on how to walk more closely with Him in our daily routine.

B. Jesus really influences the lives He touches. As Jesus reached out in love to Zacchaeus, the heart of the tax collector melted before the warmth of the love of Jesus. Surely, this is that compassion of God the prophet was speaking about when he said, "I will give you a new heart and place a new spirit within you, taking from your bodies your stony hearts and giving you natural hearts" *(Ezekiel 36:26)*. The conversion experience of Zacchaeus was complete. It was a total turning away from his old life. It was a 180 degree turn, a U-turn from his old life. He announced his conversion publicly, "I give half my belongings, Lord, to the poor. If I have defrauded anyone in the least, I pay him back fourfold."

We may now wish to examine ourselves about the need of a conversion in our own lives. The average one of us needs a conversion several times a day. Do we cling to our own will and want our way regardless of what others may want, or what God may want? Are we attached to something, or someone? Let Jesus point out to us the areas in which we need conversion, then beg for the strength and grace to say, "Yes, Lord."

C. Another thought which leaps out of this incident is the loving mercy and compassion of Jesus. Jesus knew that He would be criticized for going "to a sinner's house as a guest." That did not deter Him in any way. He stated unequivocally that He came to search out and save sinners. He is the Good Shepherd who goes in search of the lost sheep, even willing to leave the 99 in the desert to fend for themselves while He rescues the one which was lost.

Such love cannot help but touch our hearts. All He asks in return is our love. He is waiting for our response.

We bring our meditation to a close with (1) an act of thanksgiving to God for the favors and graces He has given us during our time of prayer; (2) a review of the manner in which we made our meditation in order to improve our meditative prayer the next time; (3) a final prayer asking God's blessing upon our prayer and work so that we might live out in our lives the fruits of our meditation.

Finally, we should select some thought, word, or phrase which has really spoken to us during our meditation. This thought should be written down in our spiritual journal. In this way we can more easily recall it during the day. Furthermore, writing concretizes our resolve and makes it more exact. When we return to our journal at a later date, a rereading of our thought will serve to deepen our prayer experience.

Consciousness Examen

Another form of meditation which we will find helpful in coming before the Lord each day is called Consciousness Examen. By this we do not mean an examination of conscience in which we determine how often we may have failed in a certain area of spiritual growth, or how often we did succeed in another area of our spiritual development.

One method of using the consciousness examen to punctuate our day or at the end of the day, is to reflect on how well we acted or reacted with faith, hope or love today? Or what were the moments throughout the day when we were actually aware of acting in faith, hope or love?

The consciousness examen is an ideal method of pausing to reflect and meditate upon God's goodness and His influence in our life this day. Its purpose is not merely to determine how we reacted to God's influence, but rather to pause and to recall what God did for us this day. These are precious moments and can effect real growth in our personal relationship with the Lord.

Here is the basic methodology suggested for making the consciousness examen. There are five steps. We may wish to spend more time on one step and less on another depending upon our need that day.

Enlightenment

We pray for the special grace of enlightenment. We need this grace because the examen is not simply a matter of recalling a certain part of our day. It is more than the use of our natural power of memory. We are seeking an insight by the power of the Holy Spirit. We want to transcend our human powers to look at the here and now with its limited causality and discover the Father Who loves us and Who is working in and through us. To discover His divine design in our lives, we need to use our own powers, but we also need the power of the Holy Spirit over and above our natural powers. We begin, therefore, with an explicit petition for enlightenment so that we may see ourselves as the Holy Spirit Himself sees us.

Reflective Thanksgiving

Our attitude as a Christian must certainly be one of genuine poverty of spirit. Of ourselves we are nothing as we have nothing, but we are unusually gifted by God at every moment of the day. If our attitude is not one of real poverty of spirit, we either lose many of our gifts, or we begin to make demands for things we think we deserve, or we simply take for granted all that comes our way from God. The more deeply we live in an awareness of God in our life, the poorer we are and the more gifted. Our life, then, becomes humble, joyful and filled with thanksgiving and praise.

After our prayer of enlightenment, then, we should come before God with hearts filled with gratitude, especially for those gifts which we have received during a certain part of this day. Perhaps at the time of God granting us a special gift, or acting powerfully in our lives, we were not aware

71

that this really was God's operation. As we bring ourselves to a real spirit of gratitude, it helps us to be ready to discover God's gift more clearly in a future and unexpected happening. Our gratitude should focus on a concrete, recent, and uniquely personal gift. There is so much in our lives we take for granted. As we spend time each day in our consciousness examen, God will bring us to a deeper realization that all is gift. It is right, therefore, to give Him praise and thanks!

Review of Our Actions

In the third dimension of the consciousness examen, our prime concern in faith is what has been happening to and in us since our last examen. We must ask ourselves: What has God been asking of us? Only secondarily do we consider and review our own actions. Here we must be sensitive to our interior moods, feelings, urges and movements. The examen is the chief means for discerning our interior consciousness.

Our life must first be a listening, then an acting in response. We need interior quiet, peace and great receptivity that attunes us to listening to God's Word at every moment and in every situation and only then responding by our own activity. Our first concern, then, is with these subtle, intimate, affective ways in which the Lord has been dealing with us during these past few hours. Perhaps we did not recognize His calling us in that past moment, but now in our examen our vision becomes clearer and His call becomes more apparent to us. Secondly, our concern is with our own actions insofar as they were responses to His calling. So often our activity becomes our primary concern and we lose all sense of response to His calling.

This part of the examen, perhaps more than any

other, has been misunderstood. The examen is not a mechanical approach to self-perfection by moving down the list of vices and up the list of virtues. The examen is meant to be a reverently honest, personal meeting with the Lord in our hearts.

When we become sensitive and serious enough about loving God, we begin to realize some changes must be made. Usually there is a certain area of our hearts where God is calling us especially to conversion which is always the beginning of a new life and a deeper union with Him. He is interiorly nudging us in one or other area and reminding us that if we really want to love Him above all things, we will be willing to change in this or that aspect.

The examen is a very personal, honest, and at times a subtle experience of the Lord calling in our hearts for a deeper conversion and commitment to Him.

This third dimension of the examen brings home to us a sense of our own sinfulness. This is not a guilt-laden sense of sin, but the realization that God loves us regardless of what we have done. It brings home to us a realization of our poverty before the Lord. In turn this elicits a deep sense of gratitude. As we realize that our sinfulness is wiped out by a God who wants to forgive us more than we could want forgiveness, our thanksgiving resounds from hearts filled with joy.

Sorrow

As Christians our hearts should be filled with joy and gratitude. However, our rejoicing could be quite shallow unless we have first come to a realization of our sinfulness and God's loving forgiveness. Only then can we sing our alleluias with real joy.

As we realize that the Father is calling us sinners to be His sons and daughters, we want to examine ourselves especially about the generosity of our responses to the Lord in our hearts. Our sorrow will spring from the realization of our inadequate responses. It will be a sorrow not of shame nor a depression, but an experience of the Father's desire that we should love Him with every fiber of our being. Giving expression to our abiding sorrow will be the source of genuine joy to our impoverished hearts.

Resolution

At this point in our meditative examen, we should have a great desire to look ahead with renewed vision and a resolve to be sensitive to what the Lord may call us. We should pray that we are able to recognize the subtle ways in which the Lord will attempt to communicate with us. We should ask that we may be fully alert to listen to His call with faith, humility and courage. We should be able to face the future with great hope not relying on our own power, but upon the knowledge that the Father loves us, and through His Son and by the power of His Holy Spirit He will help us to effect a fuller conversion and deeper commitment to Him. This is the source of a real supernatural hope. This will be a frightening experience at times, but one which will be joyful and exhilarating. St. Paul expresses this so aptly in the Letter to the Philippians (3:7-14), but especially in verse 13, "I give no thought to what lies behind but push on to what is ahead."

This brief outline of the Examen of Consciousness is sufficient to show that it can be an ideal method of meditative prayer. To recapture the procedure in making a consciousness examen, we see how it leads us to: (a) a prayer for enlightenment; (b) a prayer of thanksgiving to a gracious God acting in our lives; (c) a review of all our activities and God's influence on our lives; (d) sorrow and regret for our lack of awareness of God's influence and our lack of generous response to His call; and, (e) a resolve which should keep our lives attuned to His call and response.

As we faithfully continue to spend time in meditation, we will discover that our prayer is beginning to change. It is becoming more quiet. We will be using fewer words and less reasoning. When this happens some people become disturbed. They feel that since thoughts and reflections are becoming fewer, their prayer life is regressing rather than progressing. Quite the contrary is true.

Meditation frequently turns into contemplation. Meditation is a natural launching pad into contemplation. When we have reached this stage in our prayer, there is no need to form thoughts and pronounce words. We are alone with God. This, too, is gift.

Chapter Six

Praying Contemplatively

"All of us, gazing on the Lord's glory with unveiled faces, are being transformed from glory to glory into his very image by the Lord who is the Spirit" (II Corinthians 3:18).

God is a God of surprises. Perhaps one of the most startling of His surprises is the fact that He is calling us to a kind of prayer which we never dreamed possible in our active worldly existence. The Holy Spirit is inviting us into a form of prayer which is new to most of us. He is leading us into contemplative prayer.

We are aware that God has called men and women to a special vocation as contemplatives. For a long time we thought of contemplative prayer as the special prerogative of the great mystics and those persons hidden in contemplative convents and monasteries. We excused ourselves from even thinking about praying contemplatively because we felt that God was calling only certain dedicated souls to be "professional contemplatives." We thought of contemplation as being incompatible with our state in life. Now, however, the Holy

Spirit is showing us through the teaching of the Second Vatican Council and elsewhere that all men are called to holiness and this means a deeper union with God which is effected through prayer.

The fifth chapter of the *Constitution of the Church* is entitled, "The Universal Call to Holiness in the Church." As the title already suggests, this includes everyone regardless of his station in life.

The Conciliar document states this objective in these words: "The Lord Jesus, The Divine Teacher and Model of all perfection, preached holiness of life to each and every one of His disciples of every condition. He Himself stands as the author and consummator of this holiness of life, 'Be you, therefore, perfect, even as your heavenly Father is perfect.' Indeed He sent the Holy Spirit upon all men that He might move them inwardly to love God with their whole heart and their whole soul, with all their mind and strength, and that they might love each other as Christ loves them" (par. 40).

Holiness is a transformation in our lives. Genuine transformation comes most effectively through contemplative prayer. As we come to God in contemplative prayer, He is molding, shaping and forming us into patterns of holiness which we could never achieve ourselves.

In the first document which issued from the Vatican Council, the *Constitution on the Liturgy*, we find various notions of contemplative prayer suggested. We discover such expressions as "the Faithful (that is, all of us) are to "taste to their full" of the Paschal Mysteries and by the Eucharist "to be set on fire" (par. 10). This terminology is the same as that which is used in speaking of the higher forms of prayer, especially contemplative prayer.

In the *Constitution on Divine Revelation* the

Bishops assure us that "the believers" by praying with the Word of God will grow in understanding of the spiritual things they experience. Intimate understanding and the experience of spiritual things come to us in contemplative prayer.

What Is It

Contemplation defies definition because it is an experience of God. At best, words are poor vehicles of thought and this is especially true when we attempt to relate a deep and personal experience. Our attempt to describe the experience of contemplative prayer must necessarily be inadequate.

In contemplative prayer we experience a real sense of God's presence. We long to be alone with Him to taste and savor His presence. As we experience God's love overwhelming us, we strive to respond to His great love in the solitude of our own heart. We simply want to bask in His presence. We want to be exclusively for God and we want Him to be for us.

Praying contemplatively is like taking a sunbath. If we wish to take a sunbath we simply lie motionless in the sun to absorb all its warmth and let its rays nourish our whole being. We do not have to exert a muscle, simply bask in the sunshine. In contemplative prayer we are totally absorbed in His presence and rest in the warmth of His love.

In order to pray contemplatively we must come to God with genuine poverty of spirit. We must be one of His little ones — the anawim. A friend shared this thought with me about contemplative prayer. He said, "In my prayer I consider myself a little child again and I climb up into my Father's lap. I feel His strong arms about me, protecting me, loving me. I do not have to speak a word, I just rest, relax and enjoy my Father's loving embrace."

The author of *The Cloud of Unknowing* defined contemplation in these words, "Contemplation is not the pleasant reaction to a celestial sunset, nor is it the perpetual twitter of heavenly birdsong. It is not even an emotion. It is the awareness of God, known and loved at the core of one's being."

To grasp some understanding of contemplative prayer we need to reflect on various aspects of prayer. Let us look briefly at the three main stages of prayer.

First, there is vocal prayer. This is a prayer with the lips with stress on words, recited or sung. Most of the vocal prayers are formulae already written or learned. There is also spontaneous vocal prayer.

The second level we call meditative prayer, or meditation. This is a prayer of the mind. We picture, ponder, reflect and think about God and His magnificent works. With our mind we seek understanding of God's love, His power, His creation. As we meditate, our lips are quiet and the mind is active. Meditation moves us to resolution and action.

The third stage of prayer is contemplation. Contemplative prayer is more heart and not so much headwork. It is a prayer of the heart which reaches out to God's presence. In this type of prayer our lips and minds are quiet, but the heart reaches out in wordless prayer and the will seeks to be one with God. We strive to experience His presence.

Contemplation is "the awareness of God, known and loved at the core of one's being." When we seek this awareness and find it in faith, we speak of this as "acquired" contemplation; when God gives us this awareness in a real experience we speak of it as "infused" contemplation.

In these days of renewal the Lord wants us to become mature and adult Christians. As mature Christians He wants us to reach a level of contemplative prayer. We may compare the stages of prayer to the stages of our education. Vocal prayer can be compared to our primary education with reading and writing. The intermediate stage of our schooling can be compared to meditation, in which reflection on life and revelation is the main subject, at the same time without neglecting vocal prayer. The third level of our education can be compared to the beginning of contemplative prayer. This point in our prayer life is an awakening to God's presence and opening of our spirit to the workings of the Holy Spirit. Our prayer life, like our education, is not a running in circles, nor is it going off on a tangent, but it is, rather, a spiral. We build on what we have already learned and keep rising higher and higher.

Let us make another comparison. If we compare contemplative prayer to vocal prayer, we could say that in contemplative prayer, we seek an awareness of that which is contained in the words of our vocal prayer, and thus making it really and truly present to ourselves. For instance, when we say, "Our Father Who art in heaven," we go beyond the words to the awareness of His presence to us, and deep within us, and we strive to dwell and rest in that presence of our loving Father.

If we wish to compare contemplative prayer to meditation, we could say that instead of ruminating over truth in our minds and reflecting upon it, we gaze at it, and awaken ourselves to His presence within us. Father Borst draws this analogy, "Meditation could be compared to the activity that goes into making and painting a picture. Contemplative prayer is then the quiet looking at the completed picture, seeing it as a whole, becoming aware of the reality of the artist's vision which it portrays."

Contemplative prayer goes beyond words and thoughts. It reaches out to God Himself, our loving

Father, to Jesus who is Lord of our lives and the Holy Spirit dwelling within us. The reality of God goes beyond words and thoughts; hence love alone can experience this reality. The medieval author of *The Cloud of Unknowing* says, "He (God) may well be loved, but not thought. By love may He be gotten and holden; but by thought never."

St. John of the Cross says, "Contemplation is nothing else but a secret, peaceful infusion of God, which, if admitted, will set the soul on fire with the Spirit of love."

Contemplative prayer goes beyond words, which are vocal prayer, and thoughts, which are meditative prayer, and reaches out to God who is that reality toward which the words and thoughts point. In this sense, we can say that all prayer must have a contemplative quality, because vocal prayer is never just a recitation of words and meditative prayer is never just an exercise in thinking.

There are many names which are used in speaking about contemplative prayer. It has been called the "prayer of silence," "prayer of repose," "prayer of the simple presence of God," and "prayer of the heart." St. Theresa of Avila calls it the "prayer of recollection" while others name it "the prayer of simplicity." The first stage of this prayer is referred to as "acquired contemplation" which is intended by God for anyone who strives with God's grace to achieve this level of prayer. "Infused contemplation" is God's gift with little or no effort on our part other than our openness to receive. All prayer is gift, therefore, we may say "infused contemplation" is given more unexpectedly.

Benefits of Contemplative Prayer

There is only one way to become a contemplative, and that is by setting aside time every day to spend in prayer alone with the Lord. Without the practice of contemplative prayer we can never become a contemplative. No recipe book ever produced a delicious meal. The directives of the recipe must be followed by some person along with all the necessary ingredients in order to prepare a delectable dish. Time and place are those ingredients for contemplative prayer and the directives can be obtained from various writers or from a spiritual director. No amount of other prayers and occupations can bring us to contemplative prayer, nor can any other form of prayer bring us the same fruits as contemplation. If we wish to pray contemplatively, we must simply begin to pray thus each day.

In order to derive the fruits of contemplation there are certain qualities required. As we discuss the benefits derived from contemplative prayer, we will at the same time touch upon some of these qualifications.

1. In order to enter into contemplation we must relax in the presence of the Lord. This prayer involves a real search for peace. Our heart and whole being must be serene and tranquil in order to pray. We must meet God, our Father, or Jesus, our Brother, or the Holy Spirit, our Guest, where they may be found, that is, within us. God can touch us more effectively in an atmosphere of serenity and tranquility. Our hour of prayer should be a time of relaxation and rest in His presence and a time when we worship Him with our whole being.

The psalmist bids us, "Seek peace, and follow after it" *(Psalm 34:15)*. Our task, then, during this hour is to let all tensions relax, to become calm and to surrender ourselves and all our interests to the Lord. We seek this peace very gently by letting go. As tension, worry, anxiety flow from us, we turn our attention to the Lord, making ourselves aware of His presence Who is the Source and Giver of all peace. Rest in His presence as a child would rest in the tender arms of his father.

2. To attain genuine peace of heart, we must be committed to live a life of peace. This is both a requisite for, and a fruit of, contemplative prayer. Our interior peace can so easily be disturbed by the lure of the seven capital sins which are the vicious tendencies gnawing at us at all times. The chief disrupter of our peace seems to be the passion of anger.

Anger can utterly destroy our prayer. Anger includes rancor, suspicion, bitterness, resentments, or peevishness. An early spiritual writer said, "Prayer is the offshoot of gentleness and the absence of anger." Anger usually arises from an undue attachment to worldly values. The same writer says, "What, in fact, would a man have to get angry about if he cared nothing for food, wealth, human prestige and so on."

Paul admonishes us to "acquire a fresh, spiritual way of thinking. You must put on that new man created in God's image" *(Ephesians 4:23-24)*. Again he warns us, "Your attitude must be that of Christ" *(Philippians 2:5)*. We must be wholeheartedly committed to the mind of Christ as revealed in the Gospels. Jesus proclaimed His mind in the Sermon on the Mount when He told us that there was no place in our lives for violence, hatred, revenge, judging. He asked us to cultivate gentleness, compassion, willingness to give and to share generously, to love and to forgive. This can be accomplished only by the power of the Holy Spirit dwelling with us. Contemplative prayer aids us in making ourselves receptive to the influence of His divine power.

3. One of the most frequent questions asked about contemplative prayer is what value has it for my life? We are so pragmatic in our thinking that we must look for results in concrete terms before we can really appreciate the value of something. Someone has said so aptly, "In order to pray well, we must be willing to 'waste time.' "

As we pray contemplatively, slowly but surely we come to a wonderful transformation in our lives. Personally, we may not be so much aware of this transformation within us, but others will recognize it early in our attempt to pray contemplatively. If we pray day after day, month after month, our lives gradually change in ways that we might never have thought possible. Real contemplative prayer involves a receptivity to the Holy Spirit. Gradually, His gifts and fruits will be more and more evident in our lives. In contemplation we experience the Person of Jesus more really and His mentality gradually captivates us. We find ourselves at peace. Daily we are healed in the living water of His Spirit and we grow to that full stature of which Paul speaks.

Again, we call upon the author of *The Cloud of Unknowing*. He describes this transformation in a delightful manner (and remember this was said hundreds of years ago).

"All those who engage in this work of contemplation find that it has a good effect on the body as well as on the soul, for it makes them attractive in the eyes of all who see them. So much so that the ugliest person alive who becomes, by grace, a contemplative finds that he suddenly (and again by grace) is different, and that every good man he sees is glad and happy to have his friendship, and is spiritually refreshed, and helped nearer God by his company."

St. Theresa of Avila has this to say about the

effectiveness of contemplation, "If you will try and live in the presence of God for one year, you will see yourself at the end of it at the height of perfection without your even knowing it."

Let us return to our previous question: What benefits do we expect to derive from contemplative prayer? To answer, let us ask another question: What is our purpose in life? Briefly, our purpose in life is to become godlike. Jesus said, "Learn from me, for I am gentle and humble of heart" *(Matthew 11:29)* and again, "What I just did was to give an example: as I have done, so you must do" *(John 13:15)*. Then He gave us that all-embracing admonition, "I give you a new commandment: Love one another. Such as my love has been for you, so must your love be for each other" *(John 13:34)*. How can we love in this godlike manner?

Little by little we become what we contemplate. It is in contemplating God that we become like Him. Let us recall the story of Nathaniel Hawthorne, *The Great Stone Face*. Hawthorne tells us of a little village located at the foot of an immense granite mountain. Nature had hewn the likeness of a human face on the side of the mountain. The figure was imposing and huge, with a great nobility of features. According to a legend, a man of exceptional character would one day come to the village. His features would resemble those of the face on the mountain. He was to bring many blessings to the hamlet and to do much good for the inhabitants.

A child who lived in this village was fascinated by the great face on the mountain. He would spend long periods of time gazing upon the figure. Years later, after he had grown into manhood, the villagers recognized in him the one who was foretold in their legend.

Hawthorne was asked what had happened to the man that his features resembled so closely the great stone face on the mountain. Hawthorne answered laconically, "He prayed." But they objected, "He prayed, but you said he only looked at the great stone face. Do you call that prayer?" The writer replied simply, "That is all the same thing; to pray is to contemplate; and to contemplate is to become."

In the same way, if we seriously contemplate God, we will become godlike, and becoming godlike, we will think and act as God would have us think and act as Christians: we will love as God would have us love. Praying contemplatively is the most effective way of achieving this end.

4. Another powerful fruit of this type of prayer is a new freedom we enjoy. Through the action of the Holy Spirit, we become free and more truly human. Before God in prayer, we learn to see ourselves as we truly are. Most of us are not truly ourselves. We are afraid that we might not be accepted by others if we are really human and so we have learned to wear many masks. We do so much playacting and live many pretenses. As we come closer to God, and as the Holy Spirit pours His love upon us, we are happy to accept ourselves as we really are without any pretense. We are truly happy with ourselves. We become more truly ourselves because we are true before God.

This freedom will help us in our interpersonal relationships. Real Christian love means that we strive to enter sympathetically into other people's feelings and situations. This sensitivity is achieved together with true prayer. If we are genuine before God, we become true to ourselves and honest with others. How true are the words of St. John, "If anyone says, 'My love is fixed on God,' yet hates his brother, he is a liar. One who has no love for the brother he has seen cannot love the God he has not seen" *(I John 4:20)*.

5. As we enter more deeply into contemplative prayer we will discover that all our other prayers take on a new meaning and that our whole prayer life will become integrated. As we become more contemplative, we are able to give all our prayers a contemplative quality.

As we begin to pray contemplatively, we may feel the need to drop some of the vocal prayers to which we have been accustomed. We will feel an inability to merely "say prayers" hurriedly, or slovenly, without reverence or regard for their sense.

As we progress, we may discover that we may be moved to return to more vocal prayer especially those of a repetitive nature. For instance, the Rosary, or the Jesus Prayer, or the brief ejaculatory prayers take on new meaning because they help us to dwell in the presence of God.

The teachings of the Second Vatican Council also make it clear that mental prayer is really necessary if we are to profit from the Mass and other liturgical and paraliturgical functions. We are advised that priority should be given to mental prayer over a multiplicity of other prayers. The reason for shortening the Mass and the Office was to achieve a twofold purpose: to make the Mass and Office into meaningful prayers; and, secondly, to give more time for personal contemplative prayer.

Relevance

Contemplative prayer gives us the exuberance of children. Children are not preoccupied with what might have to be done today or tomorrow. They take time to enjoy the present moment. They live the sacrament of the moment.

In our day, contemplative prayer is necessary for many reasons. We need to pray contemplatively to discover the meaning of life. There are many and complex problem areas which cannot be resolved unless we come close to God in prayer and permit Him to give clarity to our vision and understanding to our heart. Our work can easily become routine, commonplace and even a drudgery. Time spent in contemplative prayer brings us to a new and deeper understanding of the theology of work as a share in God's creative power and as a service of love to our fellowman.

Leisure time, too, can be filled with nervous tension and excitement, or it may even be uninspiring and dull. We easily become bored because we are so passive in much of our leisure time.

Contemplation is one of our greatest needs. It is a reflection on the meaning of our daily experiences. It is a kind of "reading between the lines" of our activities.

In our day, our senses are dulled by too much noise, too many sights and images. These sensory impressions come so quickly and so profusely that we have little time to reflect on them. We have forgotten how to use them to satisfy the soul. Contemplation makes room for God in our minds and hearts.

Contemplation is not a selfish withdrawal from the world, nor from the activities of daily living. Some of us may have a guilt feeling if we are not actively engaged in doing something. There is no reason why we must justify ourselves with incessant activity. Paradoxically as it may seem, the more time we spend in contemplation, the more we will be able to give to others.

Contemplation helps us see the glory of God in the simple harmony of nature; the smile of a child, smelling roses, observing a cloud formation, finding expressions of joy, love, sadness in the faces of our fellowman.

We need leisure time, especially leisure of the mind, to enter into contemplative prayer. We must concern ourselves only with the occupation of the moment which is to be alone with God. We must take time out to create a certain quiet in our soul. Contemplation goes beyond concepts and images into quiet listening.

Finally, when all is said and done, the challenge of contemplative prayer is that it invites us to a very personal covenant with the Lord. It is our response to His invitation to spend one hour with Him. A daily hour of prayer is our outward response to this covenant, in which we surrender ourselves completely to the Lord and the Lord gives Himself to us. This covenant is the full flowering of our baptismal commitment. Daily we can celebrate and renew our covenant with the Lord and His people in the Eucharist, which is His New Covenant with us. A daily date with the Lord will bring an enrichment one would not dare to imagine.

Chapter Seven

Praying With Others

"Again I tell you, if two of you join your voices on earth to pray for anything whatever, it shall be granted you by my Father in heaven" (Matthew 18:19).

Jesus taught us much about prayer. He instructed us and taught us by His example about the necessity of private prayer. During the Sermon on the Mount He said, "Whenever you pray, go to your room, close the door, and pray to your Father in private" *(Matthew 6:6)*. Jesus did not imply that this was the *only* way to pray. If you read the entire section of Matthew 6:1-14, you will find that Jesus is warning us against praying for the approval of others, and telling us that there is only One to whom we should pray. Here Jesus is speaking only about the motive for prayer not about the kind of prayer.

The truth of the matter is that when we have entered into a deep relationship with God in private prayer, and when we have experienced His overwhelming love for us, we feel compelled to shout from the housetops what we have experienced in private prayer. Secondly, we need to praise and glorify God along with others. Jesus said, "What you hear in private, proclaim from the housetops" *(Matthew 10:27)*. He also encouraged us to share with others in prayer what God is doing in our lives when He said, "Whoever acknowledges me before men I will acknowledge before my Father in heaven" *(Matthew 10:32)*.

Jesus instructed us also on the need to pray with others, to pray as a group, as a family, as a community. When the disciples asked Jesus to teach them how to pray, He said, "This is how you are to pray: Our Father in heaven ... give us today our daily bread ... forgive us ... subject us not to the trial ... deliver us" *(Matthew 6:9ff)*. The plural use of "our" and "us" here shows that Jesus wanted us to pray with each other.

On another occasion He not only encouraged us to come together to pray, but He also told us how powerful our communal prayer would be. He said, "Again I tell you, if two of you join your voices on earth to pray for anything whatever, it shall be granted you by my Father in heaven. Where two or three are gathered in my name, there am I in their midst" *(Matthew 18:19-20)*.

Jesus invited His disciples to pray with Him. He invited His three favorite friends to come join Him in prayer. "He took Peter, John and James, and went up onto a mountain to pray." It was while they were praying that the marvelous transfiguration took place. "While he was praying, his face changed in appearance and his clothes became dazzlingly white" *(Luke 9:28-29)*. By His own example Jesus taught us to pray with others.

When Jesus faced His cruel passion and death, He needed the support and prayers of His disciples. He took all His apostles to the Mount of Olives and encouraged them to pray. He wanted the more personal prayer support of His three special friends, Peter and Zebedee's two sons, as He invited them to go farther into the garden to pray with Him.

The early Christians understood the necessity for coming together to pray. After the ascension of our Lord into heaven, they went back to the Upper Room. "Entering the city, they went to the upstairs room . . . together they devoted themselves to constant prayer" *(Acts 1:13-14)*. We find the early Christian community being bonded together in an atmosphere of loving concern and common prayer. St. Luke, the early Christian historian, states it succinctly, "They devoted themselves . . . to the breaking of bread and the prayers" *(Acts 2:42)*. When Peter and John were released from custody, they went back to "their own people" and together "all raised their voices in prayer" *(Acts 4:23-24)*. When Peter was miraculously released by an angel after Herod had arrested him, "He went to the house of Mary the mother of John (also known as Mark), where many others were gathered in prayer" *(Acts 12:12)*.

When the Christians in the church at Antioch were gathered together for prayer, the Holy Spirit spoke to them as a community and outlined His plans for them. "On one occasion, while they were engaged in the liturgy of the Lord and were fasting, the Holy Spirit spoke to them . . . then, after they had fasted and prayed, they imposed hands on them and sent them off" *(Acts 13:2-3)*. These are but a few of the examples of communal prayer among the first followers of the Way.

As God continues to implant the desire for prayer in our hearts, we are reaching out to discover new dimensions in our prayer life. One of the methods which is new to many of us is a form of prayer which is called by various names: "group prayer," "communal prayer" or "shared prayer."

Hereafter let us call it "shared prayer." This form of prayer is ever growing in popularity and effectiveness.

Shared prayer is usually spontaneous prayer which is used when praying with another person or with several people. It is not simply praying together with others, for instance, a group coming together to pray the Rosary, or some part of the office or community prayers. This praying together is excellent and it does help to form community and it does add efficacy to our prayer. It is a fruitful form of prayer, but it is not what we ordinarily call shared prayer.

Shared prayer is not so much "praying together" with one or more people but it is rather "praying with" others. Shared prayer, for the most part, is praying with one or several people as the Holy Spirit moves us. At the beginning, shared prayer may seem difficult and rather strange for many. However, once we have broken the sound barrier and heard our own voice praying out of the fullness of our hearts, it becomes a rewarding experience.

Fruits

The fruits of praying with others in this fashion are tremendous. In the first place, as we pray with another person we establish a new relationship with him even though we might have known him for a long period of time and think we may know him well. We usually relate to others on a superficial level. We talk about little things or "little nothings." We rarely really get to know another person until we have prayed with him regularly. In fact, there are husbands and wives who have lived together for many years who only recently have come to really know each other, and that only after they began to pray together in this way.

Secondly, shared prayer makes us aware of others. It makes us aware of their worries and anxieties, their timidity and fears, their joys and happy moments. As we become aware of another person's needs, we can better support and encourage him.

Thirdly, as we pray together it helps us understand one another better and it builds better interpersonal relationships. In prayer, we can more easily forgive another person and we can better ask his forgiveness. Praying with another person also helps us to understand his motives. It is so easy for us to misinterpret another's actions. Praying with another person brings us to a mutual understanding and builds a trust and confidence in each other.

Shared praying is an ideal way to build genuine Christian community. Praying together is the matrix which cements mutual relationships. Christian community must be built on love. Praying with another person helps us establish that bond of perfection.

Fourthly, our own life is greatly enriched as we pray with others. Another person's thoughts and words stimulate our thoughts and by the process of association we begin to experience God's presence and power more fully in our lives. For instance, if another person thanks God for his good health, it reminds us that God has also blessed us with life and health. Praying together really adds a broader dimension to our life of prayer.

Fifthly, as we support one another in prayer we derive mutual strength and encouragement for our daily living. We profit psychologically by praying with others. We know that others are sympathetic and love us on our trek along life's highway. We will find this awareness very supportive. Furthermore, who could estimate the power of prayer when the Body of Christ reaches out to the Father in fervent prayer for one another? Jesus assured us many times of the value of coming together in His name and agreeing with our brothers and sisters in prayer.

The sixth great advantage of shared prayer is a newfound freedom which we enjoy. For the most part many of us are playacting. We never reveal our true selves. As we pray together, we begin to share in love. We feel free to expose our real feelings. We feel more comfortable with others as we pray with them. We can be more genuinely ourselves. This freedom is a great blessing. We no longer have to be on our guard, nor do we fear that others may not accept us if they discover the real person we are.

Praying with others makes us even more genuine with God. Do you realize that we even try to be phonies before God? We rationalize ourselves into thinking that we are putting forth our best efforts, that we are really reaching out in love to others but as we pray with others, we see ourselves more clearly as we are — how halfhearted and selfish our efforts are.

Finally, praying together is an excellent way of giving spiritual direction and receiving spiritual direction from others. As we pray together, God speaks to us through others. In prayer, God's will for us becomes more apparent. As we pray with others, we can be a source of spiritual direction for them.

Jesus said that "you can tell a tree by its fruits." We can judge the value of praying with others by the results which this kind of prayer produces. From the few results mentioned above, the power of shared prayer is quite apparent. That is why Jesus taught us how to pray with others.

Types of Shared Prayer

There are many and diverse ways of sharing prayer. The variety of forms of shared prayer can really challenge our creative ingenuity in planning new and pertinent methods and still let us remain open to the leading of the Holy Spirit. Before we mention some methods of shared prayer, we would add a word of encouragement and one of caution. In the first place, shared prayer does not mean that we are constantly speaking to God and to one another. Shared prayer means also a shared listening. Silence is making room for God. In our prayer, there must be a time for communal listening. In these moments of silence, there can be a real experience of God's presence. The caution we suggest is that discussion is not really prayer. Discussion is valuable and can be very fruitful at times but it destroys the atmosphere of prayer. Discussion can profitably follow after the time of prayer is ended.

It may be profitable for us to examine briefly a few of the methods of shared prayer, realizing that there are many and varied forms not mentioned.

Unstructured

When two people are praying together or when there are only a few coming together, the procedure of the meeting can be informal and unstructured. Whereas the larger the group the more structure will be required. Even though the group may be small, the prayer naturally falls into two divisions: The first part of the prayer should give praise and glory to God and, in the second part of our prayer, we should minister to one another and our needs. Usually there is no appointed leader for this shared prayer.

This unstructured meeting may begin with an

opening prayer or a hymn which initiates the time of prayer. Each person may wish to praise and thank God for some blessings. He may wish to share some pertinent passage of Sacred Scripture. Perhaps a text of Scripture spoke to him and he may wish to share it with others. Even though there may be few people present, the prayer time can be interspersed with some favorite or appropriate hymns. Singing is praying and it should always be related to the theme of the prayer.

Even though prayer is primarily praising and thanking God, we want to be sensitive to the needs of others. We come together to support one another, to pray for one another. Intercessory prayer is also a way of showing Christian love. We may bring before the group the needs of someone else who is not present.

The time and place for these informal sessions can be arranged according to the wishes and needs of the group. However, there must be some degree of regularity about these meetings if we wish to deepen our prayer life together.

This type of shared prayer is ideal for husband and wife, for families, for a few men or women who work together. Fidelity to shared prayer is most rewarding.

Fourplex Plan

When a group comes together to learn to pray together and to share with each other, it is well to have some definite form or structure in which each person feels comfortable. For those who are just beginning to pray together, the structure of the prayer meeting should be simple. This fourplex plan is an easy one to follow. It is a good icebreaker and will encourage timid souls to speak out their prayer. Here is the procedure:

Each person should be encouraged to pray aloud in all four areas, even if only a brief word. This plan is uncomplicated but it does give some needed direction to our prayer.

1. Each person in turn should praise and thank God for something: His majesty, His goodness, the gift of His Son to us, His providential care of the world, His love . . . etc. The prayer can be very brief: such as, "Thank You, Father, for the gift of Your Son to us . . . Praise You, Lord, for You are a kind Father . . . I thank You, Holy Spirit, for guiding Your Church . . . "

There should be pauses between these prayers so that the impact of thoughts may sink deep into our being. These pauses are filled with the presence of God and are moments of deep prayer.

2. In the second round every person should thank God for a special personal gift to themselves, such as health, a safe trip, recovery from illness, family, work, etc. . . . This phase of the prayer may not come so easily for some people because of its personal nature. However, with some encouragement, the members of the prayer group will soon feel comfortable with one another.

3. In the third step of this type of prayer meeting, we turn to prayers of petition. We ask God for some special grace or blessing for someone else. We may pray for the Church, for our leaders in government, for members of our family and a whole host of other requests which come to mind.

4. Lastly, we ask God for some specific need for ourselves. Strange to say, this is the most difficult part of the prayer meeting. For beginners, it is difficult at times to unburden ourselves and really ask for ourselves. There is a fear of revealing the weaknesses of our true selves. Here we need great understanding and kindness. We need to be sensitive to those who find this portion of the prayer meeting

hard.

This plan of shared prayer is introductory. It will help lead us into greater spontaneity and freedom of expression. We will find it gratifying and furthermore it will create a desire for more and deeper prayer experiences.

Shared Scriptural Praying

Another form of group prayer is shared praying with Sacred Scripture. This kind of shared prayer is excellent for families, married couples, and mixed groups, young and old. It works best with groups of ten or less. When more are present, it is wiser to break into smaller groups.

Here are a few directives which will be helpful in shared scriptural praying.

1. Select a short passage from the Bible. To begin with it is wise to select an action scene from the life of Jesus or some parable. These passages are better known and lend themselves more easily to sharing.

2. The leader invites those present to relax and be comfortable and listen carefully to God's Word. He may remind those present that Jesus gave us the assurance, "Where two or three are gathered in my name, there am I in their midst" *(Matthew 18:20)*. The leader may begin with a short, spontaneous prayer aloud, such as, "Speak to us, Lord, help us listen to Your Word and to enjoy being silent in each other's presence. Move us to speak out when You want to use us to proclaim Your Word. Also teach us to remain silent when You prefer that. Teach us to speak to You and the Father and to praise You aloud uninhibitedly."

3. If the leader senses an uneasiness, or fear or anxiety, or any evil influence present, he may silently exorcise it by a simple command: "In the

99

name of Jesus be gone." Then He may call upon the Holy Spirit to fill the group with His presence and love.

4. The leader now reads the passage aloud slowly and distinctly. He should pause so that every word and phrase may sink into the hearts of the listeners.

5. After the reading, let the group listen in silence to what the Lord is saying to them. Then each in turn can share aloud what the passage or some phrase or even a certain word meant to him personally. This should always be done in the first person using "I" not "We." The shared thought should be honest and simple, not preachy, nor exhortative nor drawing lessons for others. He can express himself with such words: "I heard this. . . . This thought struck me. . . . To me it meant. . . . I felt this. . . etc."

We must be careful not to permit this prayer period to become a discussion. This would be disastrous. Discussion can be valuable, but it should follow the prayer meeting and not take place during the meeting.

We should peacefully, humbly, sensitively listen to God's Word and simply share what it said and meant to us personally.

We should feel at peace during the silent gaps between the readings and the contribution which others may make. These silent moments are golden and afford rare opportunities for letting God's message resonate and slowly deepen in us. During these silent periods relax and savor His Word or the thought someone else contributed.

When we humbly listen and honestly share the meaning and impact of God's Word upon us in this way, we exercise our gift and responsibility of prophecy for the benefit of others. A prophet is one who simply speaks God's Word or message to others. He is not one who foretells the future. If we do not share what God says to us, we are not using the gift God has given us and we are depriving others of some rich spiritual nourishment which God wishes them to receive through us.

6. After the first round of sharing, the same passage is read aloud a second time slowly either by the same reader or by someone else. This time it is a richer listening experience because the remarks each one shared have enriched the passage for others. God does speak to all present through one another and this is Christian prophecy.

A second round of sharing, usually richer and deeper than the first, follows the second reading of the passage of Scripture. If anyone feels moved to share a thought or insight, he is encouraged to do so. Furthermore, someone may feel moved to pray aloud after the second reading. He should feel free to do so.

7. The same passage is read slowly for a third and last time. Since this kind of prayer is primarily shared listening experience, we should come to it willing and expecting to listen a great portion of the time.

After the third reading, only shared prayer is spoken aloud. Sharing insights are spoken only after the first and second reading. These prayers are directed to the Father, or to Jesus or His Holy Spirit, or to our Blessed Mother, such as, "Thank You, Father, for revealing Your Word to us through Your Son, Jesus." . . . "Jesus, help me to live Your Word in my daily life." . . . "Holy Spirit, thank You for making Your home in me," etc.

There should be at least two readings of the scriptural passage with spontaneous prayer after the last reading. Three readings are usually better, especially if the group is just learning to pray together.

Praying Together

During this prayer, before, between or after the readings, anyone may invite the group to sing a favorite or suitable hymn. This adds greatly to the atmosphere of prayer.

After each person (or when most) has prayed spontaneously, one or more times, a final hymn may be sung. It is hard to limit the experience to a half hour, but we must be careful not to permit it to drag on too long so that people lose the spirit of prayer. God's presence becomes very real, especially during the prayers. While one is praying aloud, the rest are not mere listeners. They should join in the spirit of the prayer and make the prayer their own. They can either quietly, or even aloud at times, add their "Yes, Lord ... Amen to that, Jesus ... Me, too, Lord," etc.

The frequency of this shared praying with Scripture will depend upon the needs and preference of the group. For a family or religious community, surely once or twice a week is not too frequent.

This kind of shared prayer has become a real prayer experience for many. It has effected and will continue to effect some unique transformation in lives.

Charismatic Prayer

Another form of shared prayer is called charismatic prayer. This kind of communal prayer has much in common with other shared prayer groups. The distinguishing feature is the fact that those coming together to pray charismatically are open to use all the gifts the Holy Spirit gives them, such as prophecy, tongues, etc. This type of prayer is dealt with in the next chapter.

Through the Prophet Isaiah, God said, "See, I

am doing something new! . . . The people whom I formed for myself, that they might announce my praise" *(Isaiah 43:19 & 21)*. John also tells us that the One who sat on the throne said, "See, I make all things new!" *(Revelation 21:5)*. God is certainly making all things new in our day, as He is bringing us together as His people. As He places this desire in our hearts to come together with our brothers and sisters, to pray together with them, we are beginning to form genuine Christian community. We are beginning to love in a deeper way than ever before. Yes, He is forming us into a people of praise.

Chapter Eight

Praying Charismatically

"The Spirit too helps us in our weakness, for we do not know how to pray as we ought" (Romans 8:26).

When the second Vatican Council was announced hopes were running high for a great spiritual renewal throughout the Church and the entire world. In preparation for the Council, saintly Pope John XXIII asked us to do two things. In the first place he urged us to read the Acts of the Apostles reflectively and prayerfully. He suggested that we relive the time and events when the disciples gathered together in the Upper Room preparing for the coming of the Holy Spirit. Jesus had told them, "Wait, rather, for the fulfillment of my Father's promise, of which you have heard me speak. John baptized with water, but within a few days you will be baptized with the Holy Spirit" *(Acts 1:4-5).*

Secondly, Pope John asked us to pray this prayer with him, "Renew your signs and wonders in this our day as through us a new Pentecost."

God not only heard that plea but He responded

far more generously than we dared to imagine. God's response to man's need is always unique and extravagant. Through the power of His Holy Spirit, God is opening up many unexpected avenues to spiritual renewal. One of these avenues is popularly called the Charismatic Renewal in the Catholic Church.

In their *Statement on Charismatic Renewal*, the bishops of the United States said, "One of the great manifestations of the Spirit in our times has been the Second Vatican Council. Many believe also that the Catholic Charismatic Renewal is another such manifestation of the Spirit" (par. 5).

The Charismatic Renewal is not a new devotion to the Holy Spirit, nor has it been brought about through a more intense study of the doctrine on the Holy Spirit. No, it is rather an unexpected and spontaneous action of the Holy Spirit in our midst.

The Holy Spirit is effecting a spiritual renewal in our times by introducing us to a whole new life of prayer. The Spirit is creating in the hearts of countless men and women a great yearning for prayer. They are discovering a new power and richness in their prayer life which they have never before experienced. This is the very heart of renewal.

How is this being brought about? God gives us the key to the answer, "For my thoughts are not your thoughts, nor are your ways my ways, says the Lord" *(Isaiah 55:8)*. There can be no explanation other than God's mysterious action in our lives.

In the Charismatic Renewal many people have come to know God by experiencing His loving presence and power within them. This experiential awareness of God's personal presence comes to us through what we call the Baptism in the Holy Spirit.

Baptism in the Holy Spirit is itself a special gift

105

from God. It may be called a "personal ceremony" in which we renew more deeply our baptismal commitment, eagerly accept Christ the Lord in our life, and, in the name of Jesus, beg the Holy Spirit to release in us, through His powerful presence, all the graces and gifts which we have received in all the sacraments, especially the graces of Baptism and Confirmation.

It is true that we have received the Holy Spirit in Baptism and His fullness in Confirmation. The Baptism in the Holy Spirit is not a new infilling, but rather a release and an outpouring of His personal presence and power within us. It is a sort of blossoming forth of God's divine life in us.

Jesus is the Baptizer. He alone can baptize us in His Holy Spirit. John the Baptist made this quite clear, "I baptize you in water for the sake of reform, but the one who will follow me is more powerful than I. I am not even fit to carry his sandals. He it is who will baptize you in the Holy Spirit and fire" *(Matthew 3:11)*. Jesus will baptize us in His Spirit if we open ourselves to receive this gift. The first condition is the total oblation of our whole life to Him, thus making Him really the Lord of our life.

When a person prays that the power of the Holy Spirit be released in him, he discovers a number of realities in his life. In the first place a person who has been baptized in the Holy Spirit discovers that Jesus is present in the community. The Words of Jesus take on a new meaning, "Where two or three are gathered in my name, there am I in their midst" *(Matthew 18:20)*. This is the beginning of a new concept of community and it will open many new vistas in our prayer life as we shall see later on.

A second effect of this prayer for the release of the power of the Holy Spirit is an awareness of a new and vital relationship with Jesus. Many look upon the Baptism in the Holy Spirit as an experience of some mystical proportions. This is not the case. It is, rather, a deeper, more intimate relationship with Jesus. The Spirit leads us to Jesus and Jesus leads us to the Father. It is knowing at the very core of our being that Jesus is present in us. This awareness enkindles a more personal and a more loving relationship with Him. We have always believed in the presence of Jesus and of the Holy Spirit in us, but a new and deeper relationship develops with this gracious outpouring of the Spirit. It is a very intimate and personal relationship with the gloriously reigning and risen Jesus present in us through the power of the Holy Spirit. He is not a God far removed from us, but He is more present to us than He was to the Apostles before the Resurrection. There is not only a mystery involved here, but also a consoling and comforting truth. Yes, "Jesus Christ is the same yesterday, today, and forever" *(Hebrews 13:8)*.

This twofold awareness of the presence of Jesus through the power of His Spirit makes a big change in our prayer life, both in our private prayer and in group prayer as well.

In the Charismatic Renewal, the Holy Spirit is drawing us into a fuller and deeper union with Him in prayer. The desire to want to pray is itself a gift from the Holy Spirit. St. Paul assures us, "It is God who, in his good will toward you, begets in you any measure of desire or achievement" *(Philippians 2:13)*.

At this point, it is timely to ask just what do we mean by charismatic prayer? How is charismatic prayer different from other forms of prayer? Charismatic prayer is not diametrically different from other forms of prayer, in fact, it has much in common with all prayer. A person who is striving to pray charismatically is open to the operation of the

Holy Spirit in him. He is receptive to whatever gifts the Spirit bestows on him and is eager to use these gifts, as Paul repeatedly insists, for the upbuilding of the Body of Christ. The gifts found in charismatic prayer are many. Usually the gift of tongues, prophecy and inspired teaching are heard in a prayer meeting. This is one aspect of charismatic prayer which differentiates it from other kinds of prayer.

By virtue of the Baptism in the Holy Spirit, we are led to a more intense life of prayer. This is particularly true of people who were not particularly prayerful people before the release of the Spirit within them.

It will be profitable for us to review some of the distinguishing characteristics of charismatic prayer. This will also help us to understand a little better what God is trying to accomplish through the Charismatic Renewal.

Praise

The constant reverberation of praise permeates charismatic prayer in both private prayer as well as group prayer. For many of us this is a new dimension in our prayer life. We have long been accustomed to placing our needs before our Father; we readily intercede for others, and we frequently turn to God with hearts filled with gratitude. However, we have almost completely forgotten about the significance and the beauty of the prayer of praise. If we wish to ascertain how completely we have forgotten this form of prayer just scan any hymn book or manual of prayers and you will be surprised as to the scarcity of hymns or prayers which are pure praise of God.

God wants us to praise Him. The psalmist encourages us to praise God, "Offer to God praise as your sacrifice." And God responds in this same psalm, "He that offers praise as a sacrifice glorifies me" *(Psalm 50:14 & 23).*

A bishop once told a group of charismatics, "I am happy that you are in our diocese because you are leading us back to a form of prayer that we have long ago forgotten. Please continue to praise God and teach us also how to praise His majesty . . . "

The theme of praise is so much a part of charismatic prayer that the expression "Praise the Lord!" has become a common greeting.

More will be said about the prayer of praise in a later chapter.

Private Prayer

During these days of spiritual renewal, the Holy Spirit is drawing more and more people into a deeper life of prayer. After the release of the Spirit, a person experiences a great longing to spend more and more time alone with God. So impelling is this desire that many seem to be able to make time for prayer even in the midst of a busy, hurry-filled work-a-day world. As the Spirit brings us into a greater awareness of our personal relationship with Jesus, time for prayer takes on a new priority in our lives. As our heart knowledge of Jesus increases our desire to meet Him in private prayer grows proportionately. Some charismatics have a fixed time for personal prayer which they fondly call their "daily date with Jesus." The length of time for private prayer varies, but there are many who find that they can spend an hour each day alone with God.

In addition to their regular prayer time, some people punctuate their day with shorter periods of prayer. At times they snatch a few moments of their lunch hour for prayer or reflective scriptural reading. For others even coffee breaks are used for prayer. This daily walking with the Lord fills the lives of many people with a peace and joy which they have never before experienced.

One person said, "I always thought I was too busy to pray, and on this pretext, I offered my work as my prayer. However, since I was baptized in the Spirit, I find that after I give the Lord my hour of prayer, my work is no longer a drudgery and I accomplish even more than I did before when I thought I was too busy to pray. And what joy and peace!"

Secondly, we find we can pray in places which would normally not be conducive to prayer. Waiting for a bus, driving to work, or washing the dishes, are prayerful experiences for many people.

A professional man shared with us a change which has come into his life. He said, "In my business I must fly a great deal, I used to spend this time in reading unimportant things, or simply chatting about nothings with my fellow travellers. Now I find that I can put my head back on the reclining seat, close my eyes and be alone with Jesus oblivious of those around me. Of course, a celestial sunset or a beautiful cloud formation at 39,000 feet are helpful in creating a mood for prayer. For me to be able to pray this way just has to be a gift from God. I could not do it myself. I never even dreamed of doing it."

Time for personal prayer has become a precious priority in the lives of many. This is the beginning of genuine spiritual renewal.

His Word

Another characteristic of charismatic prayer is the use of the Bible. The Holy Spirit is drawing many people in the Charismatic Renewal to a genuine love for Sacred Scripture. These people have had little or no contact with the Bible previous to their new relationship with Jesus and the Father which the Spirit is effecting in their lives. After the gift of the Baptism in the Holy Spirit, there is a real longing for His Word. Charismatics are spending much time in studying the Word of God, in reading His Word reflectively and striving to pray contemplatively with Scripture.

St. Thomas Aquinas, in his monumental work *Summa Theologiae* (in the section of "Graces Freely Given") taught that Christians need spiritual gifts in order to know and understand divine revelation as set forth in His Word. God's revealed truths are beyond our power of comprehension. Consequently, Christians need special gifts to know and understand God's Word and also to be able to teach and preach these truths. We also need signs so that others may believe.

Personal Encounters

Those involved in the Charismatic Renewal are experiencing a deepening of their personal commitment to Christ. As a result they are growing in their devotion to the Eucharist and are partaking more fruitfully in the sacramental life of the Church. Daily Mass is not uncommon for those striving to live the life in the Spirit. The Sacrament of Penance is becoming a renewed and deeper personal experience of the forgiving, healing and redeeming love of Christ for them. They want to meet Him more frequently in this Sacrament of healing. Likewise Confirmation is a milestone in the life of commitment to Jesus. Jesus instructed His disciples, "See, I send down upon you the promise of my Father. Remain here in the city until you are clothed with power from on high" *(Luke 24:49).* By the light of the Spirit, we are beginning to understand that we cannot live, much less deepen our daily commitment, unless we are empowered by His Spirit. In the Sacrament of Confirmation we receive a new fullness of Spirit.

With the outpouring of the Holy Spirit within us, the Sacraments, which Jesus instituted for our salvation, take on a whole new importance. The reception of the Sacraments now becomes a deeply personal and joyous encounter with Jesus. They become wellsprings of strength and nourishment along the road of life. We find an eagerness to receive them as often as possible in order to enjoy the personal presence of Jesus within us.

Devotional Practices

Many of the former devotional practices are taking on a new significance after the Baptism in the Holy Spirit. Eucharistic devotions and the Way of the Cross are becoming personal encounters with Jesus on a real experiential and contemplative level. The Rosary, too, is becoming a contemplative experience of God's loving providence as we reflect on the events of our salvation history. Reverence for the Mother of the Lord is taking on a fresh meaning.

Tongues

In a prayer meeting, there is usually a manifestation of one or several of the charismatic gifts. The gift which attracts the most attention is the gift of tongues. A few comments about this gift may be helpful. This is not an attempt to give a comprehensive explanation of this mysterious "praying in tongues."

112

We are the temples of God and we do believe that the Holy Spirit is dwelling within us and praying in us. Sacred Scripture keeps us aware of this truth. "Are you not aware that you are the temple of God, and that the Spirit of God dwells in you?" (I Corinthians 3:16, also, cf. I Corinthians 6:19; Ephesians 2:20; II Corinthians 6:16).

Since we are not able to pray of ourselves, the Holy Spirit comes to our aid in prayer. He prays in us to the Father. "The Spirit too helps us in our weakness, for we do not know how to pray as we ought; but the Spirit himself makes intercession for us with groanings that cannot be expressed in speech. He who searches hearts knows what the Spirit means, for the Spirit intercedes for the saints as God himself wills" *(Romans 8:26-27)*.

The early desert Fathers understood this truth. They described Christian prayer as listening more deeply within ourselves to the prayer Jesus utters through His Spirit to the Father. In this sense our prayer becomes more passive. We are praying not on our own, but the Spirit, or Jesus Himself, prays in us.

When a person believes that he is really the temple of the Holy Spirit, and when he prays that the power of the Holy Spirit be released in him, he discovers that the Spirit can and does pray in him. The Spirit frequently manifests His presence by bestowing the gift of tongues. The person then begins to articulate the Spirit's prayer by praying in tongues. The gift of tongues is often called a prayer language. The person begins to yield his life to the Spirit without reservation and uses his tongue and vocal chords to praise, worship and thank the Father.

What that person already believes, is somehow experienced through this gift of tongues. St. Paul clarifies this belief in writing to the Romans. "This hope will not leave us disappointed, because the love of God has been poured out in our hearts through the Holy Spirit who has been given to us" *(Romans 5:5)*.

With this outpouring of the Holy Spirit we begin to realize the marvelous work of transformation which is taking place within us as the Holy Spirit leads us to a spirit of recollection and a deep desire for prayer.

Group Prayer

The Holy Spirit is the source of unity and the builder of community. One of the first fruits of the Baptism in the Spirit is a sense of community. Jesus founded His Church as a community. The Spirit is teaching us our responsibility to form a loving, serving community. One of the means which the Spirit is using to lead us to reach out in love to one another is the urgency to come together to form a praying community.

At the present time, the chief expression of this need for community is the prayer meeting. People come together, usually weekly, in church halls or private homes and sit in a circle while they spend an hour or two, or even three, in periods of silent prayer, the singing of hymns, spontaneous prayer, the reading of Scripture and spontaneous sharing. Someone may give a teaching. Often a teaching is contained in what one may be sharing about his or her personal experience with the Lord. Occasionally there may be a prophecy given or someone may speak in tongues followed by an interpretation. An atmosphere of quiet, peace and joy usually characterizes the meetings. We shall mention some of the characteristics as we go along.

While a charismatic prayer meeting is open to the leadings of the Spirit, nevertheless there is some form of order followed in the prayer meeting. Two distinct dimensions become evident. The first part of the prayer meeting centers on the worship of God. If the primary attention during prayer meetings is directed toward God, then spontaneous prayers of praise and adoration, songs of praise and thanksgiving, readings from the Scriptures, especially the psalms, will flow freely. In a good prayer meeting, worship of God will become the real center of the prayer meeting and will be the heart that gives life and direction to everything else.

Second, there are many ways in which the presence and action of the Holy Spirit is manifested in a prayer meeting. The primary way, which struck me forcefully and which convinced me of the authenticity of the workings of the Spirit, is the love and affection which was shown to one another. People had tried to impress me with the signs and wonders which God was working in our times. The sign which always impressed me was the loving concern shown for one another. To me, this is the real sign of the working of the Spirit.

The loving concern is shown as we pray with and for each other. If anyone has any special request, time is taken to pray with that person for his special needs or for the requests which he has brought to the group. Jesus reminds us of the importance of praying together, "Again I tell you, if two of you join your voices on earth to pray for anything whatever, it shall be granted you by my Father in heaven. Where two or three are gathered in my name, there am I in their midst" *(Matthew 18:19-20).*

A charismatic prayer meeting is characterized by spontaneous praying, interwoven with singing. Usually there is some sharing of God's Word and what it means to someone, along with some sharing of what God has done for a certain person. St. Paul outlines rather well what should go on during a prayer meeting. The first converts in Corinth were carried away with their enthusiasm and had to be corrected by Paul. He gave them this advice about their coming together to pray, "When you assemble, one has a psalm, another some instruction to give, still another a revelation to share; one speaks in a tongue, another interprets. All well and good, so long as everything is done with a constructive purpose" *(I Corinthians 14:26)*.

An evident characteristic of a good prayer meeting is joy. In fact the whole meeting is permeated with great joy which bubbles to the surface at the least provocation. This joyfulness does not exclude seriousness. No, joy is a sign of the presence of God working in His people. If real joyfulness pervades the tone and spirit of the prayer meeting and the relationship of people to one another, we can be certain that the Holy Spirit is present in His people.

Another characteristic is peace. A prayer meeting should have a tone of rest, resting in the Lord, of peacefulness, not anxiety or tension. Peace is a fruit of the Spirit. He brings this peace to the hearts and minds of those who trust completely in His presence and power in their lives. As we experience His presence in a prayer meeting, we will also know that deep down, quiet, interior peace which the world cannot give.

Singing is an important part of a prayer meeting and frequently it is a major part of the meeting. A prayer meeting is not a songfest, nor is singing just for enjoyment like a hootenanny. Singing is praying. In fact someone said that singing is twice praying. Singing as a way of prayer gives praise and worship to God.

A person who was attending her first prayer meeting was disturbed by all the singing. As she looked around the room she discovered that all had their eyes closed and the singing came from the depth of their being. Afterward she commented, "When the singing bothered me, I looked around and found that I was the only one who was singing, all the rest were praying."

In a prayer meeting the charismatic gifts are used frequently. The gift of prophecy is often evident. It is one of the teaching gifts. Prophecy is that gift by which God, speaking through a person, gives a message to an individual or to the whole community. It is God making use of someone to inform us what He thinks about the present situation or what His intention is for the future, or what God wants others to know or be mindful of right now. Prophecy is not necessarily a prediction of the future.

St. Paul was desirous that this gift be asked for and used. He speaks of it often, "Set your hearts on spiritual gifts — above all, the gift of prophecy." He goes on to explain briefly the purpose of the gift of prophecy. " . . . the prophet, on the other hand, speaks to men for their upbuilding, their encouragement, their consolation" *(I Corinthians 14:1-3)*.

Speaking out in prophecy is more than just saying something that happens to be on a person's mind. The prophet receives an anointing, an urging to speak a message from God. He realizes that he has a message from God, although often he does not know it until he actually yields to God and begins to speak. To the degree to which he yields to God, his message will be pure.

When prophecy is given at a gathering of Christians, it has a powerful effect in drawing them to God and deepening their sense of the presence of God. Prophecies are also an effective way of God directing His people. Besides the reassurance of God's infinite love for each one of us, prophecies bring us hope and encouragement. The gift of prophecy is just another manifestation of God's loving concern for each one of us on our pilgrimage back to

117

Him.

During the course of a gathering for prayer, God may call someone to give an inspired teaching — "another some instruction to give," as Paul puts it. This teaching may be an explanation or application of a Scriptural passage. It may be an explanation of some truth or some witness of God's goodness. A teaching is different from a prophecy. A person who gives the teaching does so with his own understanding. He sees the truth of what he is saying, whereas a prophet may not understand what he is saying.

In a teaching, the Spirit inspires someone to speak his understanding of a truth of the mystery of Christ. Perhaps he may have some special insight and understanding of the teaching of Jesus when He explains the relationship between the Father and the Son as in Luke 10:21-22. Another example is the first chapter of Ephesians where Paul teaches the Ephesians and us about God's plan of salvation.

An inspired teaching is a gift of the Spirit which builds up the Body of Christ. The teaching can also be an exhortation or admonition which gives guidance and direction to our lives.

Another charismatic gift which is evidenced in prayer meetings is the gift of tongues. First of all, the gift of tongues can be a gift of prayer for an individual which we mentioned earlier. This is the more common use of the gift of tongues. When the Spirit urges someone to speak out loud in tongues it is for the edification of everyone present. In this case, the speaking in tongues should have an interpretation so that the whole assembly can understand what God is doing. The experience of giving an interpretation is similar to the experience of prophecy. The interpreter, like the person who speaks in tongues, does not understand the tongues. Again we rely on Paul's teaching, "A man who speaks in a tongue is talking not to men but to God. No one understands him,

118

because he utters mysteries in the Spirit . . . If I pray in a tongue my spirit is at prayer but my mind contributes nothing" *(I Corinthians 14:2 & 14)*. In other words, the gift of interpretation is not a gift of translation. It is an urging to speak words which are given. To experience the gift of tongues and its interpretation gives one a real sense of the presence of the Holy Spirit in a gathering.

The flow of a prayer meeting is frequently punctuated with a spontaneous singing in tongues. This is also called singing in the Spirit. Voices joined in singing the praises of God can be an exhilarating and reverential experience. Again it cannot be defined or described but must be witnessed. It brings one to a sense of awe and wonder of God's presence through the power of His Holy Spirit.

The leader of a prayer meeting will often encourage the participants to raise their hearts and voices in a word of praise. Each person present prays out loud expressing his praise and thanks to our loving Father. Every person praying simultaneously swells the word of praise into a grand chorus of worship of God.

A prayer meeting is often punctuated with silent pauses. If someone has shared a teaching, or prophecy, or testimony, the presence of God may be felt so keenly that automatically everyone pauses to be alone with God. These silent pauses are filled with prayer from the heart.

These are some of the characteristics of what may happen when a group of people come together in Jesus' name to pray. Charismatic prayer is not something we do, but rather something we live. It is really a life-style initiated and supported by the Holy Spirit.

Chapter Nine

Mary At Prayer

"My being proclaims the greatness of the Lord, my spirit finds joy in God my Savior" (Luke 1:46).

Jesus taught us how to pray both by word and by example. Lest the example of Jesus seem too lofty for us to imitate, He gave us a model of prayer for our emulation. This model is a creature like ourselves. She is His Mother and ours. As a model for our own life of prayer, Mary is our exemplar par excellence. Prayer was Mary's life style.

The first requisite for prayer is a relationship with God. As we strive to establish our personal union with God, we are praying. Words are only one means of communicating with God. Words help us to strengthen and solidify this relationship, but much more is needed. We need a very personal relationship with God. A good relationship is based on attitudes, awareness of and response to one another, and a host of other factors.

On the human level, we can draw an analogy from the beautiful relationship between a mother and child. The mother and child have an intimate personal relationship with each other long before any verbal communication is possible. Only after the child grows and matures can this relationship between mother and child be broadened and strengthened through good verbal communication.

From the very first moment of her conception, Mary had a deep relationship with God since she was conceived free from all sinfulness and all evil tendencies. As she matured, the awareness of God's presence actualized within her and she responded progressively until that momentous day when the Angel Gabriel appeared to invite her into a unique and deeper relationship with God. Mary's exemption from all sin made her gracious "fiat" to the incarnation, and to her divine motherhood, possible.

We might say that Mary's value system changed as God called her into a more intimate relationship with Him. God was without a doubt Mary's number-one priority. The time she spent in prayer confirmed this conviction more and more as her unique vocation unfolded. Mary's focus was ever on God.

The same is true in our lives. The closer we come to God, the more completely we give ourselves to Him, the more radically will our value system change. What seemed important to us at one time in life now has little or no significance. As our personal relationship with God matures, He will become the first and foremost priority in our lives also.

This relationship with God is fundamental to a life of prayer.

Public Prayer

Mary teaches us several kinds of prayer. Each method of prayer is conducive to an integrated prayer life. Mary prayed publicly with the others.

Mary went regularly to the Temple to pray. Mary and Joseph took the child Jesus to the Temple to present Him to the Lord. "When the day came to purify them according to the law of Moses, the couple brought him up to Jerusalem so that he could be presented to the Lord, for it is written in the law of the Lord, 'Every first-born male shall be consecrated to the Lord.' They came to offer in sacrifice 'a pair of turtledoves or two young pigeons,' in accord with the dictate in the law of the Lord" *(Luke 2:22-24).* At this time they were active participants in the ceremony of purification. Yes, Mary prayed as she offered her Son to God. Her interior disposition of submission to the law, even though she was exempt, was in itself a prayer posture.

Twelve years later we find Mary going to the Temple. "His parents used to go every year to Jerusalem for the feast of the Passover, and when he was twelve they went up for the celebration as was their custom" *(Luke 2:41).*

As the pilgrims wended their way to Jerusalem they prayed and sang. When they caught sight of the dome of the Temple their hearts leaped with joy as they jubilantly sang the entry psalms. We can be certain that Mary's heart danced with joy as she sang the praises of God with her people. How fervently she must have entered into the temple worship. The psalms were the heart of the prayer life of every good Jew. Mary, too, prayed and sang the psalms from memory. She prayed the ritualistic prayers wholeheartedly and joyously.

It does not take much of a stretch of the imagination to conclude that the Holy Family gathered regularly for prayer in their sanctuary at Nazareth. How they must have pondered and shared the Word of God.

Mary's participation in public worship is an example for us. As we join the people of God in public worship, we are praising and thanking God for all that He is in our lives. Like Mary, our participation in public prayer will be a source of edification and encouragement to others. Public prayer is also an open demonstration of faith.

Besides building up the Body of Christ, praying with others will encourage and support us in our relationship with God and with our fellowman. Public prayer is a must for an integrated prayer life.

Communal Prayer

Mary prayed spontaneously with others. When she went to visit her cousin, "Elizabeth was filled with the Holy Spirit and cried out in a loud voice: 'Blest are you among women and blest is the fruit of your womb. But who am I that the mother of my Lord should come to me' " *(Luke 1:41-43)*.

Mary responded to this spontaneous prayer of Elizabeth with that joyous canticle which is repeated thousands of times daily around the world: "My being proclaims the greatness of the Lord, my spirit finds joy in God my Savior . . . "

Prayer from the heart comes naturally as we draw closer to God. Our heart, like Mary's, simply bursts forth in praise and thanksgiving to God. Mary's spontaneous prayers were undoubtedly frequent and fervent in the quiet of her Nazareth home.

Luke is careful to point out Mary's presence in the Upper Room after the ascension of Jesus into heaven. There she prayed fervently with the special friends of Jesus. "Together they devoted themselves to constant prayer. There were some women in their company, and Mary the mother of Jesus, and his brothers" *(Acts 1:14)*.

How ardently Mary must have prayed with them! She knew from deep personal experience the power of the presence of the Holy Spirit within her. She knew, too, that the Holy Spirit could mold this motley group into a loving messianic community. Prayer has a unique unifying power. She may have prayed, also, that they be granted the gifts of wisdom, knowledge and understanding so that they could become the pillars of that kingdom which her Son had established in time and space.

Mary's participation in communal or shared prayer points to another dimension for our prayer life. Shared prayer is becoming more popular today. It is uniting many people in bonds of love and forming them into genuine Christian communities.

Meditation

Mary is our model of meditative prayer. In meditation we apply our minds to the magnificent mysteries of God's love. We try to understand God's divine designs in order to move us to love and gratitude. Through this rational process we draw conclusions as directives for our daily living with God.

Mary practiced this type of prayer also. When the shepherds came to the hillside stable and found their Savior enthroned in a manger they "returned, glorifying and praising God for all they had heard and seen in accord with what had been told them." In the meantime, "Mary treasured all these things and reflected on them in her heart" *(Luke 2:19-20)*.

As Mary meditated upon these events, the mysterious designs of God began gradually to unravel for her as the Holy Spirit led her more deeply into her privileged vocation. This was the fruit of her meditation.

Twelve years later, the Evangelist again relates, for posterity, Mary's meditative prayer. When Jesus was lost in the Temple at the age of twelve, Mary and Joseph spent three agonizing days searching for Him. "On the third day they came upon him in the temple sitting in the midst of the teachers, listening to them and asking them questions. All who heard him were amazed at his intelligence and his answers." When His Mother asked Him, " 'Son, why have you done this to us?' 'Did you not know I had to be in my Father's house?' But they did not grasp what he said to them" *(Luke 2:45)*.

How true of us also! How often we do not understand God's plan. God's ways are not our ways, nor His thoughts our thoughts.

"His Mother meanwhile kept all these things in memory." Yes, she meditated upon these events to help her understand how she could better fit into God's plan of salvation.

Contemplative Prayer

Private prayer is an aloneness with God. Much of our prayer time must be spent with God in the solitude of our hearts. Unless we first go to God in prayer to be nourished and fed by Him, we will have very little to share with others. Here again Mary points the way by her own example.

Mary was a contemplative. Contemplative prayer is being alone with God, basking in the sunshine of His presence, feeling the warmth of His love for us. In this kind of prayer, words are not really required. At most, a quiet prayer in our heart such as, "My God, how great You are," or "I love You, too, Jesus," or "Thank You, Father." Contemplation is knowing at the core of our being that we are known and loved by God.

How happy Mary must have been to withdraw into the solitude of that sanctified home at Nazareth to be alone with her God. There she experienced His presence in her Son. Years later, when she heard her Son pray, "That all may be one as you, Father, are in me, and I in you," then she must have understood that the Father, too, dwelt in that humble abode of the backward village of Nazareth. She understood, too, the enriching presence of the Holy Spirit already at work in her.

Her hours of contemplation must have been many and frequent. These hours were filled with love, peace and joy. Mary's every heartbeat was in union with God. Her spoken words in Scripture are few indeed. Likewise her prayer for the most part must have been wordless. Words are not necessary when heart speaks to heart.

"Whenever you pray, go to your room, close your door, and pray to your Father in private" *(Matthew 6:6)*.

When Jesus gave us this directive for contemplative prayer, He was speaking not only of a physical place of quiet for prayer, but He was also referring to the sanctuary of solitude of the heart.

Praying with Scripture

A method of prayer which is growing in popularity is praying with Sacred Scripture. This kind of prayer is listening with our hearts as we read His Word. God's Word forms and molds us. It inspires, consoles and strengthens us. It transforms us. Someone has called the transformation which takes place within us when we pray with Sacred Scripture — the attitudinal adjustment hour.

Mary prayed the Scriptures. Here again she can

teach us by her example. Each year Mary and Joseph went up to the temple for the Feast of the Passover. Here they read the Scriptures, prayed and sang the psalms.

Also, we can visualize Mary, Joseph and Jesus pondering and praying the Word of God in their home. What new and awesome meaning the prophetic utterances of the Old Testament must have assumed for Mary as she experienced their fulfillment in her own Son.

When Mary poured forth her joy in Elizabeth's home, she gave evidence of her acquaintance with Scripture. Her canticle reflects the same joy which issued from the heart of Hannah many years earlier when she presented her son, Samuel, to the Lord.

When Hannah, the mother of Samuel, took her son to present him to the Lord, she said to Eli, " 'I prayed for this child, and the Lord granted my request. Now I, in turn, give him to the Lord; as long as he lives, he shall be dedicated to the Lord.' She left him there; and as she worshipped the Lord, she said, 'My heart exults in the Lord, my horn is exalted in my God. . . .' " *(I Samuel 1:27ff).*

Jesus Himself gives witness to His Mother's praying and living the Word of God. One day, as He was teaching, a woman wanted to compliment Him so she called out, "Blest is the womb that bore you and the breasts that nursed you." Jesus must have smiled His approval of this praise of His Mother, but He replied in effect that His Mother was blest not merely because she gave Him physical birth. No, He said, "Rather blest are they who hear the word of God and keep it" *(Luke 11:27-28).*

Jesus was saying that His Mother was truly blessed because she knew the Word of God and put it into practice in her life, as she permitted His Word to form and mold her.

As the Holy Spirit tells us through St. John,

127

"Happy is the man who reads this prophetic message, and happy are those who hear it and heed what is written in it, for the appointed time is near!" *(Revelation 1:3).*

As we daily pray and listen to His Word we will begin to "heed what is written in it."

Faith — A Prayer Posture

Prayer must begin, continue and end with a deep abiding faith. Faith characterized Mary's whole life. It permeated her life of prayer.

When she was asked to accept the divine maternity, she did not hesitate, nor did she ask for any assurances; she asked only one question and that was to ascertain just how God wanted to accomplish this tremendous mystery in her life. When the angel explained, "The Holy Spirit will come upon you and the power of the Most High will overshadow you. . . . " It was then that Mary stepped out in faith. Even though nothing like this was ever heard of in the annals of history, yet Mary believed. She knew that nothing was impossible with God. Then came her faith with commitment and expectancy. "I am the servant of the Lord. Let it be done to me as you say" *(Luke 1:35ff).*

At the outset of His public life, Jesus went to a wedding feast in Cana. It was here that Mary asked her Son for His first miracle — so great was her faith. As the wine was running low, Mary said to her Son, "They have no more wine" *(John 2:3).* Even though Jesus assured her that His hour had not yet come, she turned to those waiting on the table with an expectant faith and advised them, "Do whatever he tells you."

This is the kind of faith which is dynamic enough to move the mountains of doubt, fear and hesitation.

There are different levels of faith. First, that kind

of faith which accepts intellectually a revealed truth which cannot be understood; secondly, a faith that carries with it a commitment; thirdly, a faith with expectancy.

Mary's was a confident faith of expectancy. She expected her Son to do something about the wine shortage and He did.

As the poet puts it, "The modest water saw its God and blushed."

Poverty of Spirit — A Prayer Posture

As we come to prayer, our attitude is all important. Our prayer posture must be one of total dependence upon God. We must come to prayer with a poverty of spirit, recognizing our own inability even to pray. St. Paul assures us, "The Spirit too helps us in our weakness, for we do not know how to pray as we ought; but the Spirit himself makes intercession for us with groanings that cannot be expressed in speech. He who searches hearts knows what the Spirit means, for the Spirit intercedes for the saints as God himself wills" *(Romans 8:26ff).*

A humble disposition is essential for prayer. Recall the story Jesus told about the Pharisee and the tax collector. Jesus said, "Two men went up to the temple to pray; one was a Pharisee, the other a tax collector. The Pharisee with head unbowed prayed in this fashion: 'I give you thanks, O God, that I am not like the rest of men — grasping, crooked, adulterous — or even like this tax collector. I fast twice a week. I pay tithes on all I possess.' The other man, however, kept his distance, not even daring to raise his eyes to heaven. All he did was beat his breast and say, 'O God, be merciful to me, a sinner.' "

Jesus said the tax collector went home from the Temple justified but the other did not. It was the humility of the tax collector which was pleasing to God. Then Jesus concluded, "For everyone who exalts himself shall be humbled while he who humbles himself shall be exalted" *(Luke 18:9ff)*.

Our blessed Mother came to prayer with genuine humility. This was her constant prayer posture. She knew her own lowliness and attributed everything to God: "My being proclaims the greatness of the Lord, my spirit finds joy in God my Savior. For he has looked upon his servant in her lowliness; all ages to come shall call me blessed. God who is mighty has done great things for me, holy is his name" *(Luke 1:46ff)*.

Mary prayed with humility because she was always aware that everything which was happening in her and through her was taking place by the power of God. Humility must characterize our prayer life if our prayer is to be pleasing to God.

Yes, Lord

Jesus taught us to pray "Thy will be done." An acquiescence to God's will is an essential prayer posture. We must not only accept God's will, but we must also have a deep desire to do His will always, even His will of preference. We must want His will even if it leads us through the valley of misunderstanding and suffering.

Our daily prayer, like Mary's, must be, "What is it You want of me, today, Lord?"

Mary's whole life was one continual saying "yes" to God even in privation and suffering. Her acceptance without complaint of the poverty of Bethlehem, the exile in Egypt, the injustice of Calvary manifest her prayerful attitude of obedience to God.

Her heart was always in tune with God's will. This is prayer. When Simeon told Mary, "You yourself shall be pierced with a sword," she quietly accepted

130

that destiny *(Luke 2:22ff)*.

In one brief statement, without adjective or adverb, John describes Mary's posture of acquiescence on the height of Calvary. "Near the cross of Jesus there stood his mother" *(John 19:25)*. This laconic statement is filled with pathos, but it also says much about Mary's prayer life. Her heart was united with her Son's and thus in union with the will of the Father. Mary did not threaten the executioners; she did not scream at the terrible mockery of justice. No, she "stood," she had united her sacrifice in union with that of Jesus. This was all incorporated in her eternal "fiat."

Long hours of being alone with God in prayer must have taught her how unsearchable are His ways and how unfathomable are His plans.

Mary's prayer was her life. She loved intensely and that love kept her every heartbeat in tune with divine love. That is what prayer is all about.

Chapter Ten

We Praise You, We Thank You

"O Lord our God, you are worthy to receive glory and honor and power!" (Revelation 5:11).

We commonly make a distinction between prayers of praise, thanksgiving and petition. Many of us are accustomed to turn to God with prayers of petition. It is so natural to come to our loving Father with all our needs. This pleases God. As our Father, He is eager to help us, His children.

Another form of prayer is the prayer of praise. This form of prayer does not come as easily to us as prayers of petition and thanksgiving.

In Scripture, praise and thanksgiving are often united in the same movement of soul and are often found in the same text. For example, "I will give you thanks in the vast assembly, in the mighty throng I will praise you" *(Psalm 35:18).*

In Sacred Scripture, God is revealed as worthy of our praise because of all His marvelous gifts to us. As a result, praise and thanksgiving are brought together in the same passages.

If we can make a distinction between the forms of prayer, we can say that praise looks more to the person of God than to His gifts. Praise is more theocentric, more deeply lost in God. It is closer to adoration. Praise could also lead into ecstasy.

When we praise God we are riveting our attention on God alone. When we praise God for His might and His mercy we are concentrating solely on God. Our interest is not divided. We are not asking for any help, or for an answer to a particular problem. No, God alone is the object of our prayer of praise.

God wants our praise. He Himself tells us, "He that offers praise as a sacrifice glorifies me" *(Psalm 50:23)*.

Person of Praise

To praise God for Himself and His grandeur is the duty and privilege of every one of us. Praising God is the most effective way we can fulfill our obligation of loving and serving Him here in our earthly exile.

God wants us to praise and glorify Him. Our hearts and our lips should ever be raised in praising Him for what He is and for what He is doing for us. We should praise Him for His infinite goodness, for His inexhaustible patience, His compassionate mercy, His creative love, His providential care, His redeeming power. We should praise Him for the love, peace and joy which He bestows upon us. There is no end to the litany because everything we are and have has come from God. St. Paul exclaims, "How deep are the riches and the wisdom and the knowledge of God! How inscrutable his judgments, how unsearchable his ways" *(Romans 11:33)*. The psalmist admonishes us and encourages us to fulfill our duty of praise to God.

"Offer to God praise as your sacrifice and fulfill your vows to the Most High" *(Psalm 50:14)*. And again, "Praise the name of the Lord, for his name alone is exalted" *(Psalm 148:13)*.

In other words, as we strive to praise God for Himself and all His magnificent works, we are fulfilling our prime duty as Christians. God does want our praise. He revealed this thought to a modern mystic, "I, even I, God, whom people have foolishly feared and flattered for my gifts, I want love and friendship more than I want groveling subjects."

People of Praise

God is calling us to become a people of praise. Through the prophet Isaiah, God is telling us how much He wants to form us into a praising people. "See, I am doing something new! . . . For I put water in the desert and rivers in the wasteland for my chosen people to drink, the people whom I formed for myself, that they might announce my praise" *(Isaiah 43:19ff)*.

God is calling us to praise Him constantly in the quiet of our heart. He is also calling us to announce His praise among our fellowmen, especially those with whom we live and move and have our being each day. He is calling us to raise our hearts and voices in praise of His divine majesty. This is what He means when He says that He is forming a people to announce His praise. The psalmist encourages us, "Sing to the Lord a new song of praise in the assembly of the faithful" *(Psalm 149:1)*.

St. Paul also assures us that God is calling us together as a community to praise Him. In writing to the Ephesians, St. Paul says, " . . . that all might praise the glorious favor he has bestowed on us in his beloved." He continues, "He is the pledge of our inheritance, the first payment against the full redemption of a people God has made his own, to praise his glory" *(Ephesians 1:6 & 14)*.

Jesus formed His Church as a community. We, the Church, are fulfilling our mission more effectively as we become more and more a People of Praise.

A Living Sacrifice of Praise

God is calling us, and forming us, into a people of praise. This formation is taking place wondrously in the Holy Sacrifice of the Mass. When we come together to celebrate the Eucharistic Liturgy, God is drawing us closer together in a strong bond of unity. This is one of the powerful effects of the Mass.

Secondly, the Mass is the most perfect way to praise God. The Mass is a sacrifice of praise. We offer our meager praise through Jesus to the Father. This adds an infinite dimension to our prayer of praise. We are no longer striving to praise God ourselves, but in the Mass we are united with our eternal High Priest who makes our efforts a perfect hymn of praise.

We begin the Mass in a spirit of repentance. This repentance is necessary in order to praise God well. Perhaps we should first repent of our lack of praising God to the extent to which He is calling us.

In the Mass, especially in Eucharistic Prayer IV, we pray that through the power of the Holy Spirit we may be formed into a people of praise, " . . . by your Holy Spirit, gather all who share this bread and wine into the one body of Christ, a living sacrifice of praise."

St. Paul states so aptly what we are accomplishing through the Mass. "All praise to God, through Jesus Christ our Lord!" *(Romans 7:25)*.

The author of the Book of Sirach teaches us that although our praise cannot fulfill our obligation to worship God adequately, it is still the highest and best form of prayer. He begs us to praise God who is so much greater than all His works — greater by far than we can ever imagine.

"Let us praise him more, since we cannot fathom him, for greater is he than all his works."

135

He encourages us to continue to praise God even though we cannot fathom His infinity. When we reflect on God's greatness, His almighty power, His infinite love, we are simply overwhelmed and words fail us. That should not deter us, "Lift up your voices to glorify the Lord though He is still beyond your power to praise."

What we can see and imagine of God's infinity is very limited because our human comprehension cannot fathom God's immensity. Our minds cannot grasp the divine designs in everything about us regardless of how immense or how infinitesimal. However, *Sirach* urges us to continue our hymn of praise to God, "For who can see him and describe him? or who can praise him as he is? Beyond these, many things lie hid; only a few of his works have we seen" *(Sirach 43:33-34)*.

As we become a People of Praise, the exciting joy of living and knowing the infinite grandeur and beauty of God will know no bounds.

Alleluia

One of the richest expressions of praise is the beautiful exclamation, "Alleluia." This exclamation is used extensively in all Christian worship especially during the Easter season.

The word "Alleluia" is a compound word made up from several different words. It is derived from the Hebrew word "Hallel" which means to praise in song. The letter "u" denotes the second person plural, while "Iah" is an abbreviation for the name of God, Yahweh, the Lord God. Alleluia = Hallelu-Yah = Praise Yah (weh).

Alleluia is a word which introduces many of the psalms.

"Alleluia! Praise the Lord, all you nations" *(Psalm 117)*.

"Alleluia! Give thanks to the Lord, for he is good" *(Psalm 118)*.

St. John used this exclamation of praise in the Book of Revelation, for example (chapter 19).

"Alleluia! Salvation, glory and might belong to our God. . . . " *(verse 1)*. And again: "Once more they sang Alleluia!" *(verse 3)*. Again: "Alleluia! The Lord is King, our God, the Almighty!" *(verse 6)*.

There are many popular chants being sung today using this striking exclamation of praise. We are beginning to use Alleluia more extensively as an expression of praise to our loving and gracious God.

God of Praise

In Sacred Scripture we find songs of praise, bursting with enthusiasm, multiplying words in an attempt to describe God and His grandeur. These songs speak of God's greatness and goodness *(Psalm 145)*, of His love and fidelity *(Psalm 89)*, of His might *(Psalm 29)*, of His wonderful plan *(Isaiah 25)*, of His mighty deeds *(Psalms 104 & 105)* to mention only a few.

From the works of God, we are brought back to their author, our loving and gracious Father. "Great is the Lord and highly to be praised!" *(Psalm 145:3)*. "O, Lord, my God, you are great indeed! You are clothed with majesty and glory" *(Psalm 104:1)*.

These hymns of praise in Sacred Scripture also celebrate the great name of God. "Glorify the Lord with me, let us together extol his name" *(Psalm 34:4)*. "I will extol you, O my God and King, and I will bless your name forever and ever" *(Psalm 145:1)*. "O Lord, you are my God, I will extol you and praise your name" *(Isaiah 25:1)*.

In the New Testament praising God consists first of all in solemnly proclaiming His greatness. Here are some examples, "My being proclaims the greatness of the Lord" *(Luke 1:46)*. "Therefore I will praise you among the Gentiles and I will sing to your name" *(Romans 15:9)*. " . . . and every tongue proclaim to the glory of God the Father; Jesus Christ is Lord!" *(Philippians 2:11)*.

These are but a few of the many references in Sacred Scripture proclaiming praise to God and urging us to raise our voices to extol His name.

As we pray His Word daily, we will soon be formed into persons of praise. As more of us learn to praise God, then we will become a people of praise.

Thank You, Lord

Since God is so good to us, it is obvious that we must respond in gratitude for all His blessings. God does want our prayer of thanksgiving. He wants us to come to Him with hearts filled with joy and gratitude.

We, ourselves, have need to express our gratitude. Psychologists tell us that nothing is really our own until we have expressed it in words. As we thank God in our prayer, our gratitude becomes more intense.

Jesus taught us by His own example that we must be grateful to God. Twice the Evangelist tells us He gave thanks to His Father at the first multiplication of the loaves. "Jesus then took the loaves of bread, gave thanks, and passed them around to those reclining there . . . near the place where they had eaten the bread after the Lord had given thanks" *(John 6:11-23)*. Jesus again gave thanks at the second multiplication of the loaves. "He took the seven loaves and the fish, and after giving thanks he broke them and gave them to the disciples, who in turn gave them to the crowds" *(Matthew 15:36)*.

Jesus did the same at the Last Supper. "Then, taking bread and giving thanks, he broke it and gave it to them, saying: 'This is my body to be given for you' " *(Luke 22:19).*

Jesus again gave thanks at the tomb of Lazarus before He restored Lazarus to life. Jesus prayed, "Father, I thank you for having heard me" *(John 11:41).*

By His example, Jesus taught us how important it is to express our gratitude and appreciation to God daily for His benevolence. As creatures, we have a solemn obligation to offer our thanks to God for His manifold blessings. He is giving us life and breath at this very moment. Every heartbeat is a special blessing from God.

Give Thanks to the Lord

We know from personal experience how pleased we are when someone is grateful for what we do. God, our Father, is likewise pleased when we, His children, turn to Him with grateful hearts. When we express our gratitude it enriches our own life and makes us even more aware of God's goodness to us.

When we ponder all that God is doing for us, we are overcome with gratitude and along with the psalmist are compelled to say, "How shall I make a return to the Lord for all the good He has done for me?" *(Psalm 116:12).* "Let all your works give you thanks, O Lord, and let your faithful ones bless you" *(Psalm 145:10).*

Jesus taught us how important was our expression of gratitude to God. When He cured the ten lepers who came to Him, only one returned to express his gratitude. The other nine could have been excited and anxious to run home to their families and friends from whom they had been isolated for so long. Regardless of the reason, Jesus expressed His disappointment. "Were not all ten made whole? Where are the other nine? Was there no one to return and give thanks to God except this foreigner?" *(Luke*

Jesus also warned us against a false type of gratitude. God wants us to be sincere in thanking Him. He does not want empty words. Again Jesus taught us a valuable lesson when He told us about the Pharisee and the tax collector who went down to the temple to pray. Jesus told us how futile was the prayer of the Pharisee because he gave thanks with his lips and not his heart. "I give you thanks, O God, that I am not like the rest of men — grasping, crooked, adulterous — even like this tax collector." Jesus said of the difference of the prayer of these two men, "This man (the tax collector) went home from the temple justified but the other did not" *(Luke 18:9ff)*. When we recognize our total dependence upon Him, and when we come with childlike thanks, God is pleased with our prayer of gratitude.

Thanksgiving

We cannot have a true celebration without a memorial. As we recall some important event, person or place, only then can we celebrate a memorial.

Thanksgiving Day is a memorial of God's loving, providential care. It brings to mind God's infinite bounty to us from the days of the Pilgrims down to our very own. Likewise, Sacred Scripture is not only a record of God's infinite bounty, but also a summons for us to render thanks to God.

One of our human failings is to take so very much for granted. How seldom we say, "Thank You," even though our hearts are grateful. We know from experience how deeply ingratitude can wound.

How generous is God in bestowing His gifts upon us . . . life, breath, health, family and friends. How plenteous and rich are our harvests not only for our sustenance, but for our enjoyment as well. We need to pause to recount His loving, providential care. As we pray His Word, we are reminded of His bounteous gift to us.

The Scriptures also remind us that God wants His children to thank Him. On numerous occasions Jesus taught us by His example as He turned to His Father in thanksgiving.

What greater gift is there than His Son and the divine life which He shares with us! How tremendous the gift of His Spirit dwelling within us! How gracious His love!

Render Constant Thanks

The Epistles in the New Testament give us an insight into the attitude which every Christian must have. St. Paul diligently guides us in forming a proper Christian mentality. Repeatedly he tells us we must be grateful. He says, "Name something you have that you have not received" *(I Corinthians 4:7)*. Obviously, we have nothing which we have not received; therefore, one of our duties is to be grateful to God for all His benefactions.

St. Paul encourages us to "pray in a spirit of thanksgiving" *(Colossians 4:2)*, and to "render constant thanks" *(I Thessalonians 5:18)*. He tells us that every Christian should have a heart "overflowing with gratitude" *(Colossians 2:7)*.

Faith is a gift from God. He has bestowed that gift upon us. In our Baptism, He invited us to become members of His family. He adopted us as His sons and daughters. This gives us our true dignity as a person and a Christian. Since faith is a gift from God, St. Paul tells us we should always be "giving thanks to the Father for having made you worthy to share the lot of the saints in light" *(Colossians 1:12)*. St. Paul epitomizes much of this attitude when he says "thanks be to God for his indescribable gift" *(II Corinthians 9:15)*.

Paul Thanks God

St. Paul taught us in many different ways how to live a Christian life. He taught us that we must be grateful to God at all times.

In the introduction to nearly all his Epistles, he expressed thanks. This expression serves as an admonition to us to do the same.

Paul was grateful to God for the gift of faith given to the Romans, "First of all, I give thanks to God through Jesus Christ for all of you because your faith is heralded throughout the world" *(Romans 1:8)*.

The Corinthians were especially dear to Paul. He was thankful for God's gift to them, "I continually thank my God for you because of the favor he has bestowed on you in Christ Jesus. . . . " *(I Corinthians 1:4)*.

The same note of gratitude permeates Paul's letter to the Philippians, "I give thanks to my God every time I think of you — which is constantly, in every prayer I utter" *(Philippians 1:3-4)*.

St. Paul was grateful to God for all his co-workers. Many times he thanked God for everyone of them. He reminds Timothy of his gratitude to God for, "Timothy, my child whom I love," and "I thank God, the God of my forefathers whom I worship with a clear conscience, whenever I remember you in my prayers . . . as indeed I do constantly, night and day" *(II Timothy 1:2-3)*.

Paul also tells us that, "All Scripture is . . . useful for teaching . . . and training in holiness" *(II Timothy 3:16)*. Thus we learn gratitude from the example and attitude of the great Apostle of the Gentiles.

With joyous hearts let us sing, "Praise and glory, wisdom and thanksgiving and honor, power and might, to our God forever and ever, Amen" *(Revelation 7:12)*.

Chapter Eleven

Prayer Potpouri

Pray Always

Prayer is by no means limited to words only. In fact, words are rather poor vehicles for our deepest thoughts and feelings. An old axiom has it, "Actions speak louder than words."

Our actions, too, are prayers. When our activities are in harmony with what God wants of us at a particular time, and when they are offered in union with Jesus, then these activities become prayer. God is pleased with this attitude of prayerfulness.

St. Paul encourages us to express our gratitude to God by our actions. "Whatever you do, whether in speech or in action, do it in the name of the Lord Jesus. Give thanks to God the Father through him" *(Colossians 3:17)*. In another Letter, he says, "The fact is that whether you eat or drink — whatever you do — you should do all for the glory of God" *(I Corinthians 10:31)*.

Jesus also taught us that our good deeds are not only prayer for us, but they can even lead others to prayer. "Your light must shine before men so that they may see goodness in your acts and give praise to your heavenly Father" *(Matthew 5:16)*.

In the story of the last judgment, Jesus told us how He would consider actions such as feeding the hungry, giving drink to the thirsty, etc., if done with the proper motive. "I assure you, as often as you did it for one of my least brothers, you did it for me" *(Matthew 25:40)*.

Scripture also tells us, "Prayer and fasting are good, but better than either is almsgiving accompanied by righteousness" *(Tobit 12:8)*. Our generous sharing of God's gifts with others is also prayer.

Activity can be prayer provided that activity is begun in prayer, motivated by prayer, performed in love. Jesus lived a very active life for the three years of His public life. However, all His activity was interspersed with personal prayer. He prayed before all the important events in His life, before choosing the apostles, before raising Lazarus, in the Garden of Olives, on the Cross.

The activities of our life must frequently be punctuated with times of prayer. Our prayer will always give the proper direction to our action. Jesus said, " . . . unless the grain of wheat falls to the earth and dies, it remains just a grain of wheat" *(John 12:24)*. To work with this attitude of mind is foreign to our human nature; hence the need for the proper formation of attitude in prayer.

Jesus laid down a condition for discipleship when He said, "Whoever wishes to be my follower must deny his very self, take up his cross each day, and follow in my steps" *(Luke 9:23)*.

This condition for discipleship requires time spent in daily prayerful reflection to remind us that all our activity must be supported by prayer. A cross is formed when our will runs perpendicular to God's will. Prayer alone can bend our will to run parallel to the will of our loving Father. This is what Jesus

144

taught us by His example of setting aside time frequently for prayer, whether it was long before dawn, or spending the whole night in prayer.

Again, we say, "Lord teach us to pray" by making all our daily activities "a living sacrifice of praise."

Childlike Prayer

Repeatedly Jesus assures us, " . . . unless you change and become like children, you will not enter the kingdom of God" *(Matthew 18:3)*. This pertains in a special way to our prayer. The Father's heart is open to all His children's needs. Little ones, the anawim, conquer the Father's heart by their childlike attitude. Children come before their father with confidence and trust and lay their smallest needs before him. We must do the same with our heavenly Father. This pleases Him very much since we come in all simplicity and in loving trust.

Jesus, speaking of a human father, says, "If you, with all your sins, know how to give your children what is good, how much more will your heavenly Father give good things to anyone who asks him!" *(Matthew 7:11)*.

When we come to the Father with a childlike attitude of love and confidence, our prayer is pleasing to Him. Rest assured that He will not only grant our prayer, but His response will come with surprising rapidity and generosity.

It may happen that at times, God may not seem to answer our prayer as soon as we expect. It could be that there may be a specific obstacle hindering our prayer, such as a resentment, an unforgiving heart, a self-centered request, to mention only a few. If the Father does not seem to answer our prayer, it could be that He is teaching us how to come to Him with the proper dispositions.

Many of our needs may not seem to be given us by

God because we may not be sufficiently childlike in our approach to our loving Father. As St. James puts it, "You do not obtain because you do not ask" *(James 4:2).*

His Will

Jesus was always deeply concerned about doing the will of His Father. Repeatedly He told us that He had come to do what the Father asked of Him. On one occasion He said, "Doing the will of him who sent me and bringing his work to completion is my food" *(John 4:34).* "As is written of me in the book, I have come to do your will, O God" *(Hebrews 10:7).*

This is an all-important attitude for us to have as we come to prayer. We must seek and do the will of God. Time spent in quiet reflection and meditation reveals to us what God wants of us. As we listen to His word we can then more easily discern and discover what God is asking us to do. This is real prayer. It is sitting at the feet of Jesus and listening with our hearts to what He is saying to us.

The will of God for us is not always easy. On the contrary, it may cause a great deal of pain at times. Nevertheless, as we spend time in prayer, we find the strength to accept whatever His will is in our regard.

Here again, our Lord gives us the example. In the Garden of Gethsemane, when the vision of all the suffering which lay ahead crushed Jesus to the ground, He prayed, "Father, if it is your will, take this cup from me; yet not my will but yours be done." The Evangelist goes on to say, "In his anguish he prayed with all the greater intensity" *(Luke 22:42-44).* This prayer of Jesus teaches us a valuable lesson. Jesus prayed "with all the greater intensity" because of the overwhelming fate which awaited Him.

146

We must come to prayer prepared to seek and accept the will of God in all things. In such a prayer there is real peace. If we have spent time in prayer and have experienced God's loving presence in our lives, then we know that no fate can befall us which the Father does not either will or permit for our own good. Prayer helps us develop this attitude as a life-style.

When the will of God seems to crush us for the moment, we, too, must pray with greater fervor. Therein we will find strength. Yes, and we will even find joy as we take up our cross daily with Jesus and trudge along in His footsteps. A daily rendezvous with God in prayer will transform us to such an extent that we are prepared to meet all these exigencies of daily living.

Hindrances

It is easy for us to place roadblocks along the pathway leading to prayer. Frequently, we are not even aware of their existence. It is only when we come to recognize these barriers that we are able to remove them and pave the way to an indepth prayer life. Holy Scripture clearly mentions obstacles to prayer.

"Lo, the hand of the Lord is not too short to save, nor his ear too dull to hear. Rather, it is your crimes that separate you from your God, it is your sins that make him hide his face so that he will not hear you" *(Isaiah 59:1-2)*.

One attitude which deals a death blow to our prayer is that of pride and self-righteousness. A person who is gifted and well satisfied does not find himself in a situation where he has to come to the Father to ask for anything. Perhaps he is talented and does not feel any need for God's help. He may claim to be a self-made man who does not have to rely

147

on anyone. Indirectly, he is saying, not even on God. Such an attitude is tragic. It will soon lead to misery and unhappiness.

God wants us to come as little children to ask Him again and again because He is our Father and like any Father, it is a joy for Him to do good and give us His gifts.

"On that day you will ask in my name and I do not say that I will petition the Father for you. The Father already loves you because you have loved me" *(John 16:26-27).*

The New Testament mentions several sins which are obstacles to prayer. This means that there are definite prerequisites for prayer and if these are not fulfilled, our prayer life will suffer to say the least.

In the first place, any transgression against the Ten Commandments endangers our prayer life. A refusal to forgive others can hamper our prayer life and render our prayerful relationship with God in-effectual. Jesus warned us about this unforgiving attitude, "If you do not forgive others, neither will your Father forgive you" *(Matthew 6:15).* To forgive others is not always easy, but it is a necessary prerequisite to prayer. Yes, we must be willing to forgive seventy-times-seven, just as our Father continues to forgive us.

Another gross impediment to advancing in prayer is anger and dissension. Paul advises his protegé Timothy, "It is my wish, then, that in every place the men shall offer prayers with blameless hand aloft and free from anger and dissension" *(I Timothy 2:8).* In other words, Paul is saying that anger and dissension, of which we have not yet repented, render our prayer void and empty.

St. Peter encourages us to step out in faith and remove all mistrust and fear from our heart as we come to prayer. "Therefore do not be perturbed; remain calm so that you will be able to pray. Above all, let your love for one another be constant, for love covers a multitude of sins" *(I Peter 4:7-8).*

Greed and avarice are obstacles to God's response to our prayer. Jesus said, "Give, and it shall be given to you. Good measure pressed down, shaken together, running over, will they pour into the fold of your garment. For the measure you measure with will be measured back to you" *(Luke 6:38).*

The beloved Apostle assures us that a clear conscience is a prerequisite for an answer to prayer. He writes, "Beloved, if our consciences have nothing to charge us with, we can be sure that God is with us and that we will receive at his hands whatever we ask" *(I John 3:21-22).*

The psalmist, too, assures us that God will answer the prayers of the just.

"Turn from evil and do good; seek peace, and follow after it. The Lord has eyes for the just, and ears for their cry" *(Psalm 34:15).*

These words may cause us some concern. Who of us can claim such holiness that God will hear our prayer. God's Word does not mean that only people who have never sinned will be heard. No, it is impossible for us mortals to live without sinning. Our human nature is so prone to sin.

Scripture is speaking about the sinner who is willing to turn from his sinful ways. A decisive obstacle to answered prayer is unrepented sin to which a person clings. When sin is forgiven we can pray with a humble and repentant heart. The promise Jesus made to the tax collector is a promise to all of us. "The other man, however, kept his distance, not even daring to raise his eyes to heaven. All he did was beat his breast and say, 'O God, be merciful to me a sinner.' Believe me, this man went home from the temple justified but the other did not. For everyone who exalts himself shall be humbled while he who humbles himself shall be exalted" *(Luke*

18:13-14).

A materialistic attitude is a gross obstacle to prayer. The philosophy of materialism makes man a little god. Its criteria of success are fame and fortune. A man is esteemed or respected only by what he has accomplished or by the fortune he has amassed. There is no place for God in this mentality.

It is obvious that this attitude is not conducive to genuine prayer. Jesus says, "Seek first his kingship over you, his way of holiness, and all these things will be given you besides" *(Matthew 6:33).* Jesus is assuring us that as we strive to grow in holiness everything else will be given to us without our asking.

Jesus also warns us about seeking only material success and possessions. "What profit would a man show if he were to gain the whole world and destroy himself in the process? What can a man offer in exchange for his very self?" *(Matthew 16:26).*

Those who are imbued with this philosophy of materialism soon become enslaved by it. All their time and talent, their energy and their every waking hour are consumed in pursuit of these neostandards which are diametrically opposed to the standards given us by Jesus.

Jesus gave us the Magna Carta of Christian living when He taught us the Beatitudes. These Beatitudes are just a further explanation of His admonition, "Seek first His Kingship over you." This is an ideal prayer posture.

Do Not Be Afraid

One of the essential attitudes of mind in coming before the Lord in prayer is an attitude of trust and confidence. We are God's children and we come before Him Who is our loving and kind Father. In prayer there is no place for fear.

We are dominated by so many fears; fear of rejection, fear of failure, fear of our unworthiness in coming before God. Each time there is an encounter with the supernatural there is also a quiet, reassuring caution not to be afraid. When the angel appeared to Mary, he said, "Do not fear, Mary" *(Luke 1:30).* To the shepherds the angel said, "You have nothing to fear!" *(Luke 2:10).* When Jesus was on His way to raise the daughter of Jairus, He said to the official, "Fear is useless. What is needed is trust" *(Mark 5:36).* When the apostles saw Jesus walking toward them on the water, they were terrified. "Jesus hastened to reassure them, 'Get hold of yourselves! It is I. Do not be afraid!' " *(Matthew 14:27).*

On another occasion Jesus assured us, "Do not let your hearts be troubled. Have faith in God and faith in me" *(John 14:1).*

If we truly love God, we will come to Him in prayer with confidence and trust. He is a Father who wants to provide all the needs of His children. Jesus gently invites us, "Come to me, all you who are weary and find life burdensome, and I will refresh you" *(Matthew 11:28).*

Furthermore, John tells us, "Love has no room for fear; rather, perfect love casts out all fear" *(I John 4:18).*

Praying with genuine trust and confidence brings real peace and joy to our fearful hearts. With joyous hearts let us join the psalmist in thanking our loving Father who removes all fear and timidity from us as we reach out to Him.

"I will give thanks to you among the peoples, O Lord, I will chant your praise among the nations, For your kindness towers to the heavens, and your faithfulness to the skies. Be exalted above the heavens, O God; above all the earth be your glory!" *(Psalm 57:10-12).*

Victory Over Death

Prayer is a relationship with God. As we spend more time in prayer this relationship deepens and becomes more intimate.

Praying with Sacred Scripture draws us into a personal relationship with our loving, gracious Father. He reveals Himself as a kind, loving God Who provides for us at every moment of our existence. He is a compassionate God Who wants to forgive us more than we could even want to be forgiven.

His guiding hand leads us along our pilgrimage back to Him — our Father. He gave His Son Who is " . . . the way, the truth, and the life" *(John 14:6).* He did not leave us orphans, but gave us His Holy Spirit to abide with us to nurture, guide, strengthen and sanctify us by remaining with us and within us, sharing His divine life with us even now during our earthly pilgrimage.

As our relationship grows deeper in prayer, then death takes on a whole new dimension. Death is not to be feared; it is rather the doorway into our Father's arms.

Because of his personal relationship with God through prayer, Paul could cry out, "O death, where is your victory? O death, where is your sting?" *(I Corinthians 15:54-55).*

In speaking of our victory over death, St. Paul says, "Thanks be to God who has given us the victory through our Lord Jesus Christ" *(I Corinthians 15:57).*

Paul On Prayer

"Be filled with the Spirit, addressing one another in psalms and hymns and inspired songs. Sing praise to the Lord with all your hearts. Give thanks to God the Father always and for everything in the name of our Lord Jesus Christ."

(Ephesians 5:18)

"Rejoice in the Lord always! I say it again. Rejoice! Everyone should see how unselfish you are. The Lord is near. Dismiss all anxiety from your minds. Present your needs to God in every form of prayer and in petitions full of gratitude. Then God's own peace, which is beyond all understanding, will stand guard over your hearts and minds, in Christ Jesus."

(Philippians 4:4-7)

"Pray perseveringly, be attentive to prayer, and pray in a spirit of thanksgiving."

(Colossians 4:2)

LINGER WITH ME
Moments Aside With Jesus $2.95

Rev. Msgr. David E. Rosage. God is calling us to a listening posture in prayer in the desire to experience him at the very core of our being. Monsignor Rosage helps us to "come by ourselves apart" daily and listen to what Jesus is telling us in Scripture.

PRAYING WITH SCRIPTURE
IN THE HOLY LAND:
Daily Meditations With the Risen Jesus $2.45

Msgr. David E. Rosage. Herein is offered a daily meeting with the Risen Jesus in those Holy Places which He sanctified by His human presence. Three hundred and sixty-five scripture texts are selected and blended with the pilgrimage experiences of the author, a retreat master, and well-known writer on prayer.

DISCOVERING PATHWAYS TO PRAYER $1.95

Msgr. David E. Rosage. Following Jesus was never meant to be dull, or worse, just duty-filled. Those who would aspire to a life of prayer and those who have already begun, will find this book amazingly thorough in its scripture-punctuated approach.

"A simple but profound book which explains the many ways and forms of prayer by which the person hungering for closer union with God may find him." **Emmanuel Spillane, O.C.S.O., Abbot, Our Lady of the Holy Trinity Abbey, Huntsville, Utah.**

Order from your bookstore or
LIVING FLAME PRESS, Locust Valley, N.Y. 11560

THE BORN-AGAIN CATHOLIC $3.50

Albert H. Boudreau. This book presents an authoritative Imprimatur treatment of today's most interesting religious issue. The author, a Catholic layman, looks at Church tradition past and present and shows that the born-again experience is not only valid, but actually is Catholic Christianity at its best. The exciting experience is not only investigated, but the reader is guided into revitalizing his or her own Christian experience. The informal style, colorful personal experiences, and helpful diagrams make this book enjoyable and profitable reading.

THE JUDAS WITHIN
An Interpretation of the Character of Judas and the Judas Within Each of Us. $1.95

Rev. Kenneth J. Zanca. The key message of the book is: Accept the Judas within. In so doing, we confront the incredible mystery of God's love, a love so great that it can embrace the darkness in Judas and in ourselves.

MOURNING: THE HEALING JOURNEY $1.75

Rev. Kenneth J. Zanca. Comfort for those who have lost a loved one. Out of the grief suffered in the loss of both parents within two months, this young priest has written a sensitive, sympathetic yet humanly constructive book to help others who have lost loved ones. This is a book that might be given to the newly bereaved.

Order from your bookstore or
LIVING FLAME PRESS, Locust Valley, N.Y. 11560

REASONS FOR REJOICING
Experiences in Christian Hope $1.75

Rev. Kenneth J. Zanca. The author asks: "Do we really or rarely have a sense of excitement, mystery, and wonder in the presence of God?" His book offers a path to rejuvenation in Christian faith, hope, and love. It deals with prayer, forgiveness, worship and other religious experiences in a learned and penetrating, yet simple, non-technical manner. **Religion Teachers' Journal.**

FINDING GRACE AT THE CENTER $2.50

Abbot Thomas Keating, o.c.s.o., Basil Pennington, o.c.s.o., and Thomas E. Clarke, S.J. A book, valuable to those who have already tried to establish a prayer life, contains the following chapters: Centering Prayer — Prayer of Quiet; Cultivating the Centering Prayer; Contemplative Prayer in the Christian Tradition; and Finding Grace at the Center.

MARY:
Pathway to Fruitfulness $1.95

John Randall, STD., Helen P. Hawkinson, Sharyn Malloy. Mary is shown to be an exemplar of fruitful Christian living in her role as model relative, suffering servant and seat of wisdom. Her growing role as mediator between Catholics and Protestants is also highlighted.

THE BOOK OF REVELATION:
What Does It Really Say? $1.95

Rev. John Randall, S.T.D. The most discussed book of the Bible today is examined by a scripture expert in relation to much that has been published on the Truth. A simply written and revealing presentation.

ENFOLDED BY CHRIST:
An Encouragement to Pray $1.95

Rev. Michael Hollings. This book helps us toward giving our lives to God in prayer yet at the same time remaining totally available to our fellowman — a difficult but possible feat. Father's sharing of his own difficulties and his personal approach convince us that "if he can do it, we can." We find in the author a true spiritual guardian and friend.

SOURCE OF LIFE:
The Eucharist and Christian Living $1.50

Rev. Rene Voillaume. A powerful testimony to the vital part the Eucharist plays in the life of a Christian. It is a product of a man for whom Christ in the Eucharist is nothing less than all.

SEEKING PURITY OF HEART:
The Gift of Ourselves to God
illus. **$1.50**

Joseph Breault. For those of us who feel that we do not live up to God's calling, that we have sin of whatever shade within our hearts. This book shows how we can begin a journey which will lead from our personal darkness to wholeness in Christ's light — a purity of heart. Clear, practical help is given us in the constant struggle to free ourselves from the deceptions that sin has planted along all avenues of our lives.

UNION WITH THE LORD IN PRAYER
Beyond Meditation to Affective Prayer Aspiration and Contemplation
$1.00

Venard Polusney, O. Carm. *"A magnificent piece of work. It touches on all the essential points of Contemplative Prayer. Yet it brings such a sublime subject down to the level of comprehension of the 'man in the street,' and in such an encouraging way."*
Abbott James Fox, O.C.S.O. (former superior of Thomas Merton at the Abbey of Gethsemane)

THE PRAYER OF LOVE . . .
The Art of Aspiration
$1.95

Venard Polusney, O. Carm. *"It is the best book I have read which evokes the simple and loving response to remain in love with the Lover. To read it meditatively, to imbibe its message of love, is to have it touch your life and become part of what you are."*
Mother Dorothy Guilbuilt, O. Carm., Superior General, Lacombe, La.

LIVING FLAME PRESS
BOX 74, LOCUST VALLEY, N.Y. 11560

Quantity

_____ **Linger With Me — 2.95**

_____ **Praying With Scripture in the Holy Land — 2.45**

_____ **Discovering Pathways to Prayer — 1.95**

_____ **The Born-Again Catholic — 3.50**

_____ **The Judas Within — 1.95**

_____ **Mourning: The Healing Journey — 1.75**

_____ **Reasons for Rejoicing — 1.75**

_____ **Finding Grace at the Center — 2.50**

_____ **Mary, Pathway to Fruitfulness — 1.95**

_____ **The Book of Revelation — 1.95**

_____ **Enfolded by Christ — 1.95**

_____ **Source of Life — 1.50**

_____ **Seeking Purity of Heart — 1.50**

_____ **Union With the Lord in Prayer — 1.00**

_____ **The Prayer of Love — 1.95**

NAME _____

ADDRESS _____

CITY_____ STATE_____ ZIP _____

☐ Payment enclosed. Kindly include $.60 postage and handling on order up to $6.00. Above that, include 10% of total up to $20. Then 7% of total. Thank you.